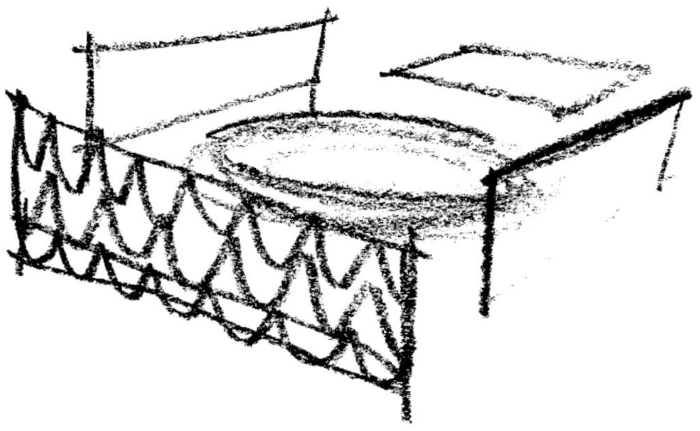

PATTERSON	HOUSES OF AOTEAROA

with more than 200 illustrations

Thames & Hudson

For Andres Arcila-Rivera and my fellow directors Andrew Mitchell and Davor Popadich

CONTENTS

FOREWORD

HERBERT YPMA

In the mid-1980s, I was young enough and naive enough to start an Antipodean 'design and architecture' magazine, called *Interior Architecture* ... from scratch. I was the publisher, the editor and the sole proprietor ... a fancy way of saying 'chief cook and bottle washer'. Surprisingly, the magazine proved to be a success, and in its fifth year of publication I opted to expand our editorial horizons. Once a year, we (the team had grown to about a dozen people by then) would produce an issue that would go further afield – to look where no one had looked before. I know this sounds obnoxiously '*Star Trek*ish', but it explains how and why I first stumbled across the work of Andrew Patterson. In an issue devoted entirely to 'Design in the South Pacific', Andrew – barely out of his twenties – was the 'star' architect.

To me, his work embodied everything that is important about architecture. It is not about pretty shapes or stylish furnishings. Nor is it about slavishly adhering to the latest trend. Inspiring architecture should make you say 'I want to go there ... I want to stand there ... I want to look out at that view ... and I will never tire of doing so!' Timeless, emotive architecture is about understanding the history, the culture and the landscape of a particular place and incorporating all of it into a new end product. Andrew Patterson does this better than anyone, especially on his home turf.

Land is a dominant factor in Polynesian culture. For Māori, land is sacred and the physical landscape commands a respect bordering on worship. Patterson reflects this perspective in his work ... and in his words: 'The landscape of New Zealand envelops us,' he says, 'it invites us to nestle in its folds, to be enveloped in the bosom of her majesty.'

And how! I challenge anyone to gaze at the photos of some of the monumental houses that are featured in this sumptuous volume and not, at the very least, utter the word – Wow!

INTRODUCTION

ANDREW PATTERSON, ARCHITECT

I grew up in the heartland of New Zealand and the first 'architecture' that I remember liking was on the roof of the local meat-processing works during a summer holiday job: huge sculptural chiller units against the blue sky. I'd sketch them during breaks. Already I knew I wanted to be an architect.

Architecture wasn't much in New Zealand and my father was determined I should be a doctor, so he sent me to Dunedin University. Dunedin is in the south of the South Island and as far as you can get from where I wanted to be – at architecture school at the top of the North Island. Entry for medicine was an A average, for architecture a B+. It was difficult, but by careful underachievement I was able to get into architecture.

I arrived back home to apologize to a disappointed Dad, only to find he had bought me a drawing board. Not just any drawing board either, but the Range Rover of drawing boards. It looked like a dentist's chair and I still use it today, much to the curiosity and amusement of anybody under thirty in our studio. Emblazoned on it was Dad's secret to life, Jacob Bronowski's book *The Ascent of Man*, the humanist as scientist.

When I entered architecture school my grandfather was ninety. He had fought at Passchendaele, surviving one of New Zealand's darkest days at war. His hobby was translating Latin. I asked him about the ancient Roman tests for good architecture, as written by the architect Vitruvius: '*firmitas, utilitas, venustas*', typically translated as 'firmness, utility, delight'. He told me that *venustas* was not the word for delight or beauty per se, but rather the word used specifically for the delight of the natural world. Architecture needs to be beautiful in the same way that the natural environment is beautiful.

Geyser is a sustainable, Six Green Star-rated, commercial complex set around two courtyards. It is one of a series of 'Cloud' buildings designed by the practice. Rather than architecture being designed simply as a response to cultural and physical issues, these projects explore ideas in the Maori creation story of Rangi and Papa. For example, the sculptural form of Geyser and even some of its environmental systems (such as the double-skin façade, which uses convection currents for ventilation, heating and cooling) are designed to mimic the dynamic relationship between the earth and the sky.

New Zealand's natural beauty is admired worldwide, but beautiful buildings have been few and far between. What we have in abundance are elements such as the grand natural amphitheatres on the North Island's volcanic plateau, forest plazas encircled by pillars of wood deeply carpeted by ferns, and beautiful underwater rooms corniced in reefs and floored in white sand, with castles of rock punching out of the sea towards the sky.

My grandmother's holiday house was near the burial place of the Tainui canoe (a migratory canoe carrying the forefathers of several of the central North Island *iwi*, or tribes) at Kawhia and I've always considered myself Ngati Pakeha (native-born New Zealander of European descent). She taught me the truth of an old Māori proverb: '*He aha te mea nui o te ao?*' What is the most important thing in the world? '*He tangata, he tangata, he tangata.*' It is people, it is people, it is people.

I want to thank all of our great clients, some of whom have come to us time and time again. You have taught us that good architecture is about longevity. To be truly sustainable a building has to endure, and for it to endure it needs to be attractive to future generations.

When Thames & Hudson approached me wanting to do a book on our work, I was thrilled at the opportunity to share. The only stipulation was that the work be residential. Since we also create many interesting commercial and civic buildings, I have included a few here in order to widen the context in which our houses are viewed.

There was also, naturally, a limit to the number of homes we could include. I've based the selection primarily on what will add up to a cohesive colour palette. I apologize for the ones we had to leave out.

Please enjoy the work. I hope these projects demonstrate our willingness, passion and love as we explore creating environments for people.

The Len Lye Centre is a single-artist gallery in New Zealand's Taranaki province, housing the work of the internationally significant artist Len Lye. Its design is based on ideas of whānau, or people, in relation to its purpose of housing the work of artist Len Lye (1901-1980). Our design for the building is generated from the identity of Len Lye himself. The building is like a person or identity rather than just an object. This is intended to create a sense of belonging and intimacy.

THE OPPORTUNITY OF NEW ZEALAND

'Last, loneliest, loveliest, exquisite, apart'

Rudyard Kipling, 'The Song of the Cities' (1922)

Around halfway between the Equator and the South Pole, all alone in the ocean at the end of the earth, you will find New Zealand.

Unchallenged, the natural world here has evolved more slowly than in other places. Diverse botanic landscapes thrive as they have since prehistoric times, under a sky so clear at night that it is impossible to count the stars.

Māori who first settled these islands called them *Aotearoa*, 'Land of the long white cloud', for that was their first clue that their long journey might be over.

Aotearoa's benign climate is diverse: from a cool sub-Antarctic in the south to a wet and warm subtropical in the north. This diversity has enabled a strange wildlife and flora to exist. Flightless birds, prehistoric lizards and native plants can still be found.

Here we have one of the most beautiful and diverse natural environments there is.

ABOVE Mitre Peak and Sinbad Gully, Milford Sound, c.1905. (Birch, A.E.: Scenic negatives and prints taken by Thomas Pringle. Ref: 1/1-003294-G. Alexander Turnbull Library, Wellington, New Zealand)

Maori believe that humanity is descended from the earth – that people are related to the mountains, lakes, rivers, seas, trees and birds. They belie he earth. Everything that lives on earth is a child of the union of Ranginui and Papatūānuku, the Sky Father and the Earth Mother. We are created in their embrace.

We do not need to draw a distinction between 'man-made' and 'natural'. Everything is one.

We share *whakapapa* (genealogy) with the natural world. We are kin. Not only are we responsible for the earth, we are part of it. And the earth is part of humanity. It is not owned by us, it is something we have borrowed from our children.

This is *kaitiakitanga*: guardianship.

ABOVE Pātaka (Māori storehouse) at Whakarewarewa, photographed 1950s. (Ref: 1/2-116897-F. Alexander Turnbull Library, Wellington, New Zealand)

S E A S C A P E R E T R E A T

BANKS PENINSULA / 2014

Our very first drawings of Seascape consisted of the simplest form of human habitat: a fire in a cave. Completed, it is no more than a porch, a living/sleeping area and a bathroom. The floorplan is the interlocking geometry of both the close view of the cove it is in and the faraway view of the Comb – a rocky outcrop that was originally a double arch, but that was sadly reduced to a single rock spire by the 2010 and 2011 Christchurch earthquakes.

Situated on Banks Pensinsula, on Te Waipounamu (the Māori name for the South Island), Seascape is a tiny beachside cottage. Rather than imposing itself on the surrounding landscape with a designated form or shape, the house is generated by the landscape itself.

The cottage's programme called for a romantic hideaway suitable for any weather and accessible only by farm track or helicopter. A place where couples can be intimate with not only one another but nature as well. Where the roar of the ocean takes the place of the demands of the outside world.

Banks Peninsula was formed by two overlapping Pliocene shield volcanoes, and the cottage itself is constructed from the very same basalt quarried from nearby. Partially set into a rock escarpment, the structure is reinforced to protect occupants from falling debris. After all, an earthquake has already altered the view, and the tiny South Pacific cove is strewn with boulders and buffeted by storms rising up from the Antarctic.

The project incorporated extensive reforestation and revegetation and Seascape is fully self-sufficient. Our hope is that it almost could have been there forever.

PAGES 18, 23-25 AND OPPOSITE We conceived of Seascape as a romantic retreat for couples who want to experience connection with nature. The cottage is totally secluded at the end of a 5 km-long (3 mile) farm track on an exposed coast. Through the design we explored the classic castaway experience adapted for the modern world.

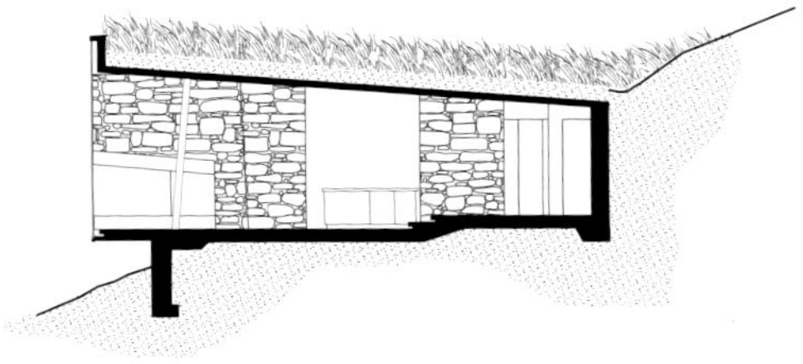

CROSS SECTION

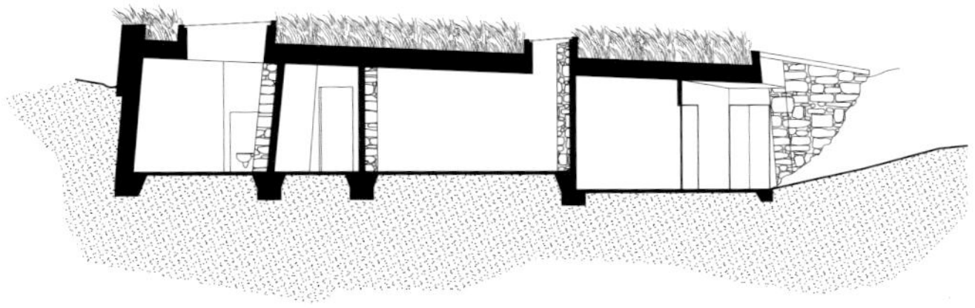

CROSS SECTION

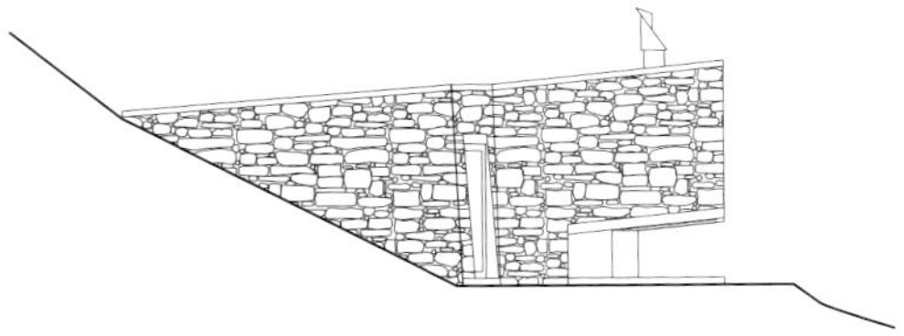

EAST ELEVATION

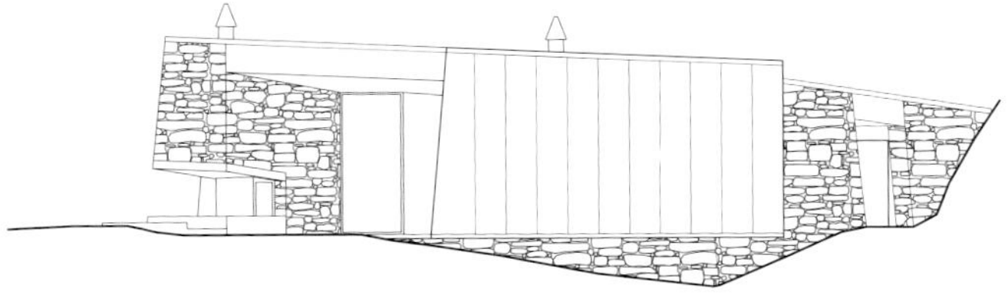

NORTH ELEVATION

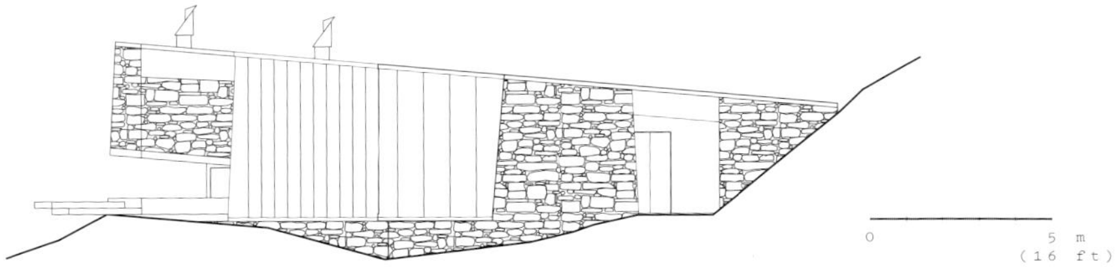

WEST ELEVATION

PLAN

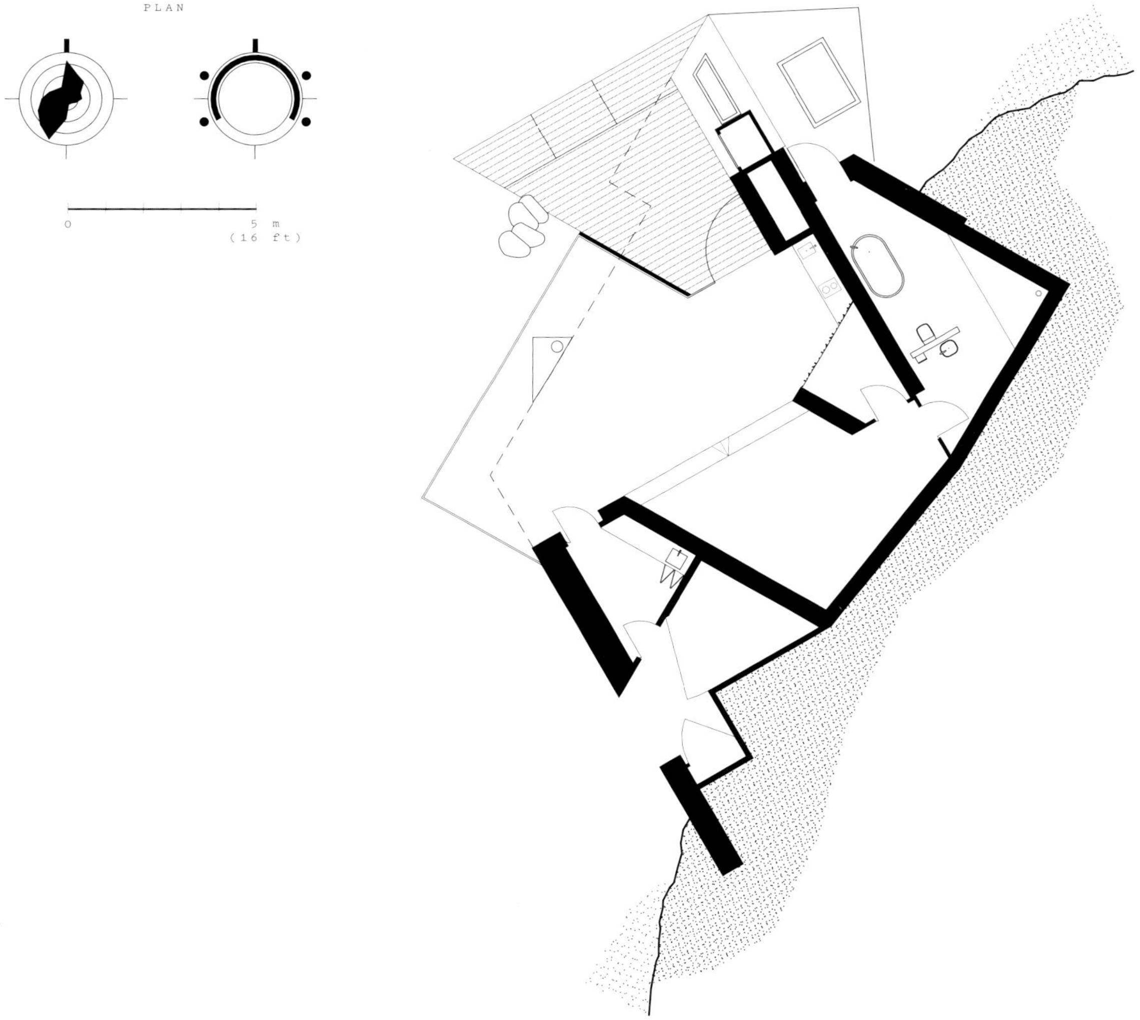

OPPOSITE AND ABOVE The weather arriving from the Antarctic is seen through a triple-glazed, steel-framed viewing wall fitted into a simple cave-like form. **FOLLOWING SPREAD** The cottage's outdoor fireplace and terrace aligns with the Comb, a well-known rock formation and navigation marker that sits against the sea horizon. The Comb used to have the form of three linked arches but collapsed to a single spire during the 2011 Christchurch earthquake.

The cottage's bedroom space looks over the living room and out to the Comb rock formation. The roof above is thick, poured-in-situ reinforced concrete designed to protect occupants from debris that could fall from the volcanic escarpment above during earthquakes.

ABOVE AND OPPOSITE The cottage is in the castaway tradition – a cave, a fire and a place to sleep. The plan combines the geometry of two views set at 30 degrees to each other: one is of the cove itself, the other of the Comb. This is about connecting people to both views. **FOLLOWING SPREAD** Marine life is abundant here; seals and sea lions, rare Hector's dolphins and bird life can be seen in the cove almost daily and provides great entertainment. The design for the cottage is just another natural pattern on the shoreline.

SCRUBBY BAY

BANKS PENINSULA / 2013

On an expansive sheep and cattle station, nestled in a dramatic natural amphitheatre, you will find Scrubby Bay farmhouse. This is an archetypal double-gable form fully clad with rough-sawn cedar boarding. It blends in with the surrounding sun-bleached hills – not unlike driftwood that has been washed onto the beach by the cold currents of the Southern Ocean.

This is a retreat commissioned by an expatriate New Zealander to create a 'home base' where the many activities the station and the coast offer can be discovered and enjoyed. The only way in is by farm track or helicopter. The secluded retreat accommodates up to a dozen people in two master bedrooms and a bunkroom. Timber storm shutters close the building while it waits loyally between visits.

Entry to the house is through a sheltered leeward porch into the central living area and here guests are confronted by the dramatic view of the horseshoe-shaped bay. At the heart of the building is a central dry stack fireplace constructed from rock quarried on the station, while throughout, macrocarpa timber with traditional rustic detailing lines the walls and is juxtaposed against refined black custom steel fittings.

The furniture is also custom designed: Mah Jong sofas and handmade rugs made from wool farmed on the land warm the home. Outside, a sunny deck extends out from the living room. Here you might find the occupants lounging, enjoying the warmth of the outdoor spa or firepit while taking in the never-ending horizon of the ocean.

PREVIOUS SPREAD The farmhouse is a rugged, utilitarian home where you can wear your gumboots or hiking boots inside and not worry about chipping the walls or marking the floors. It is used as a base for farming activities such as mustering, calving and lambing, as well as for exploring the rich sea life on the surrounding coast. Its approach access can be seen above. **OPPOSITE** The form of the house is made up of two simple gables and inspired by a historic shepherd's cottage situated on the farm. The design for the home is a contemporary model of the original cottage.

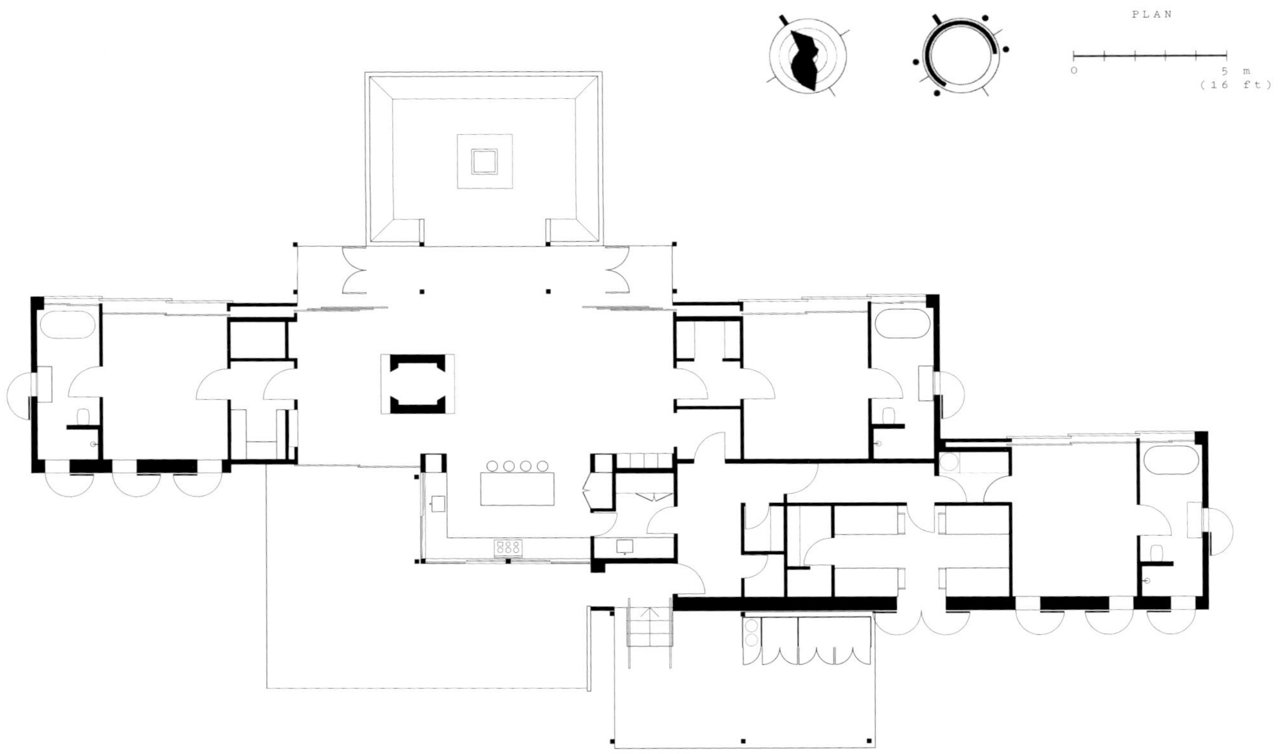
PLAN
0
5 m
(16 ft)

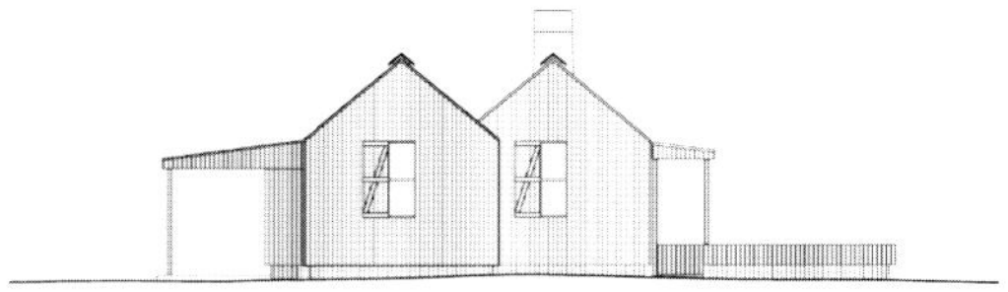

CROSS SECTION

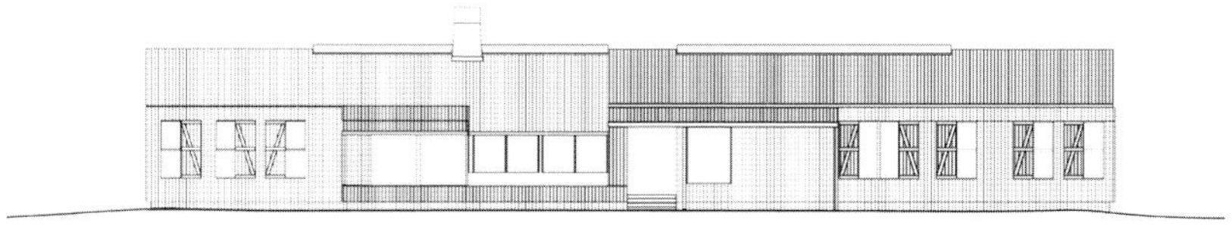

EAST ELEVATION

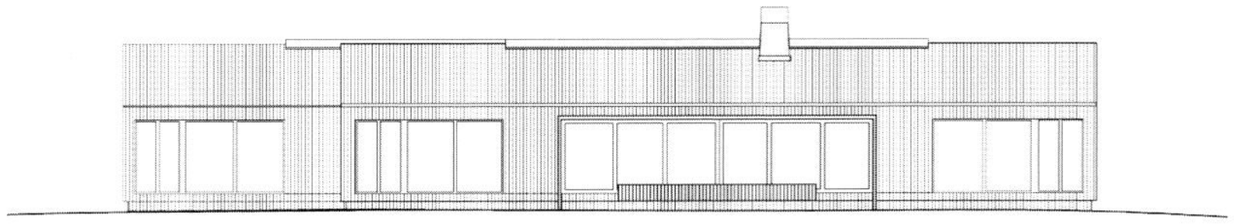

NORTH ELEVATION

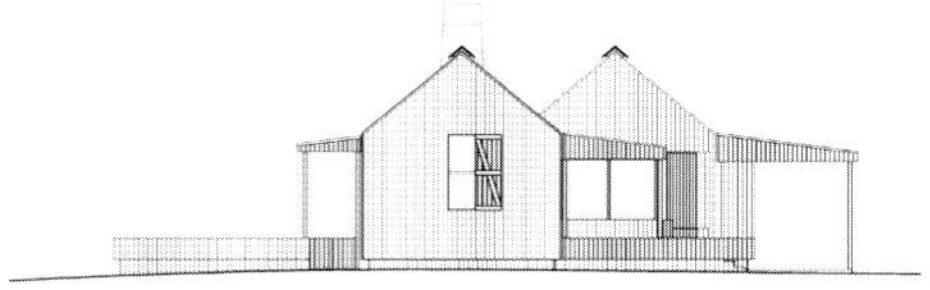

CROSS SECTION

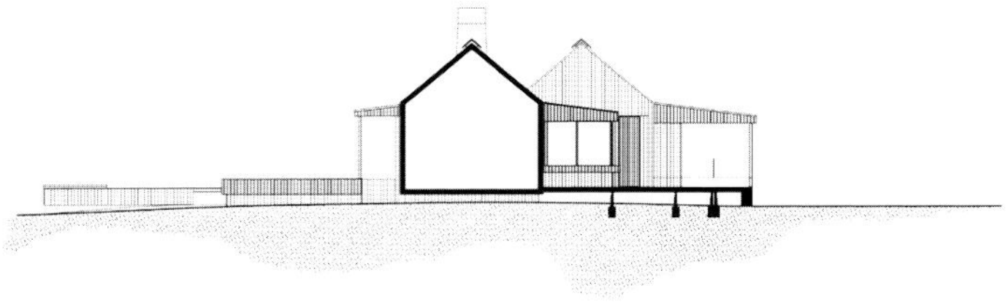

0 5 m
(16 ft)

WEST ELEVATION

ABOVE View of the house and the bay from the hills above. **OPPOSITE** The inland view from the house. The home and its colour, form and concept are patterns of the surrounding landscape and the historic farm that it is part of. **FOLLOWING SPREAD** The steel-trussed windmill is a water tower. It was here before the house and we left it in place.

The three separate bedroom wings can be blacked out with a combination of hinged and sliding storm shutters and closed up during storms or when not in use. The roof and sidings are clad in sustainably harvested western red cedar, which will silver as it ages like the driftwood on the beach.

OPPOSITE AND ABOVE The interior of the home is lined in sustainable macrocarpa timber milled nearby. The main fireplace's stone is hewn from the farm quarry. Fittings and fixtures are all bespoke. The stud height at the ridge beam is over 6 metres (20 feet). **FOLLOWING SPREAD** Scrubby Bay sits as the main actor, centre stage in this natural amphitheatre. It is the spot you would most likely gravitate to if you stumbled upon this deserted bay. It suggests that people (and their homes) can be a natural part of the planet in harmony with everything else.

BETHELLS BEACH

AUCKLAND / 1996

The part of the old volcano on which this project sits is an isthmus separating three wild black-sand beaches.

It is a remote spot, where the surf of the often ferocious Tasman Sea pounds the shore constantly. A system of sea caves, passable only on rare calm days at low tide, provides a link between two of the beaches. When it is not calm, these ancient caves breathe and crash with the ocean swells. During a storm, you hear them howling.

The client is one of the pioneering families of the area and the isthmus itself has passed down through the generations. Eighty years ago, before council rules were imposed, a small cottage was erected on the site. In 1989, during a lightning storm, it burned down. A twist in regulations allowed 365 days to design, obtain consent for and rebuild the structure before the right to occupy would be gone forever.

The brief was simple: exactly the same area and position. The first month we spent thinking. Almost 360 degrees of views were available and begging to be seen, so it really had to be an oval speaking to the old volcano, deferential in tone, more than just a model of the environment: a homage with a concrete, fireproof core hidden inside sacrificial, replaceable storm shutters.

Inside, there is one oval 'great room', two sleeping rooms and a bathroom buried into the ground behind. Each segment of the oval responds to a different beach or forest view. When opened wide the cottage becomes one outdoor covered terrace where the breeze can drift through.

This building throws its occupants into the landscape and then wraps up into a cave when needed. It is a pattern of the landscape it occupies. The family is from Bethells Beach and this is their legacy for generations to come.

PREVIOUS SPREAD AND OPPOSITE A system of sea caves runs under the isthmus on which the house is sited. The house can be shut down with thick timber storm shutters into a warm, cavelike space, echoing the caverns below.

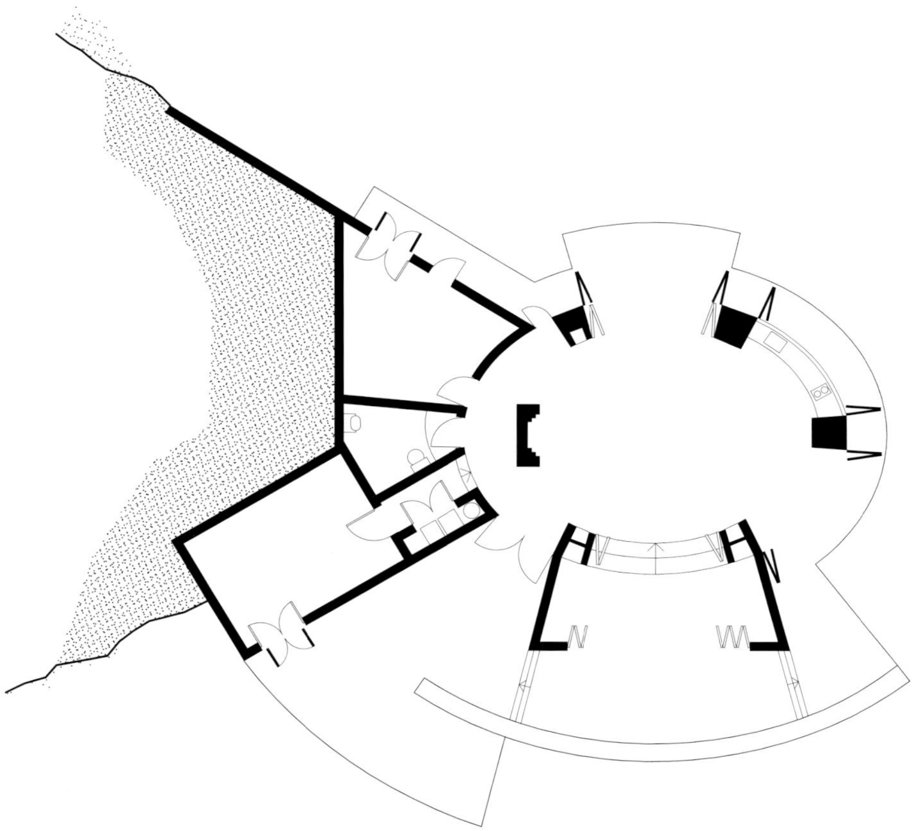

PLAN

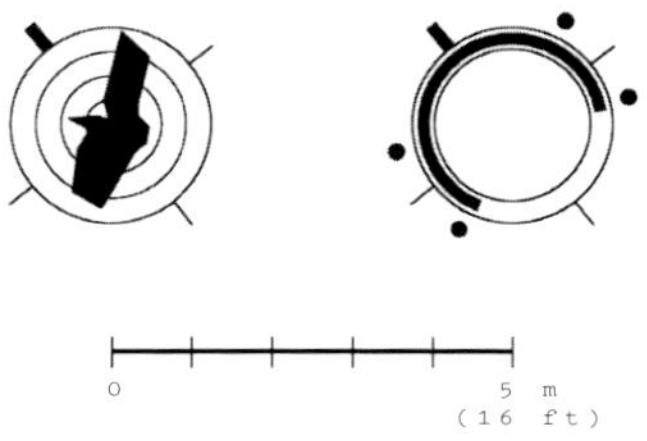

OPPOSITE The cove below the house runs with surf on most days; it is accessible only via the sea caves, which are passable at low tide.

The environment outside is as important as the interior. The 'great room' forms a simple retreat at the core of the house and folds out to the surrounding environment.

The shutters fold back and open the oval-shaped house up, transforming it into a pavilion on fine days. Each section of the pavilion opens to a different beach view.

ABOVE The home's master bedroom faces a tiny chute-like cove accessible only by a sea cave, which runs with huge surf in storms. **OPPOSITE** A view on the hike to the house that can only be accessed at low tide. **PAGES 68-70** This home sits on the part of an old volcanic cone that forms the isthmus between three black sand beaches. The beaches are linked by a system of sea caves that eroded deep underneath the cone. It is located on a small plot of private land surrounded by public parkland. All flora and fauna are native.

BELONGING

He kākano ahau i ruia mai i Rangiātea.

I am a seed that was sown in the heavens of Rangiātea.

Architecture, particularly residential architecture, is an extension of our physical presence; it is what links us to our environment.

A New Zealand Warrior in his Proper Dress, & Compleatly Armed, According to their Manner.

When we feel like we belong, we feel connected, we feel present and we have clarity. When we do not feel this sense of belonging, we can experience disconnection, confusion, even alienation and loneliness.

Underpinning the work of the Patterson studio is the idea that if our design feels like it belongs naturally to a place, to the world, to our time and culture, then it follows that the people who live there will feel a sense of belonging and connection too

At its most elemental level, architecture is about manipulating a landscape or cityscape to create environments for people. Stones are moved to provide a sheltering hearth, more stones are gathered and you have a building facing the sun's warmth. Eventually, you have moved enough around to create a village, and then a town.

Judaeo-Christian ideas have dominated Western architecture. The Judaeo-Christian story of creation has humans and the earth on which they exist made separately. The evolution of structures is thought of as man-made rather than as something that comes about naturally.

Over time, our human histories and relationships with the environment have changed, changing also the way we respond to our surroundings, how we assess them and how we design them. In the twenty-first century, as the planet continues to evolve, we find the place we occupy on earth becoming somewhat of a chicken and egg scenario: we might be a product of our environment, but more and more the environment is a product of us.

Innovation. Culture. These are dynamic inputs. Our contemporary environments, especially in urban settings, can threaten ecological and human connections. They force us down different roads.

ABOVE A pattern model of Ranginui and Papatūānuku, the Sky Father and the Earth Mother.

MAI MAI

AUCKLAND / 2007

vero
ASB

In inner-city Auckland, high on a ridge surveying the city, sits Mai Mai house. It began with a love story. The idea for Mai Mai was to create a private retreat for two distinct personalities – a hunter and a bird – and in so doing, create a singular sense of belonging for both.

A white fibreglass façade is carved with an abstracted feather pattern, inspired by the feather cloak traditionally worn by Māori chiefs. At night, this transforms into a screen as changing images and feather patterns are projected onto it.

Inside, a small footprint, there are many spatial experiences, including wide city views, a nest-like den and a garden courtyard.

Mai Mai is the story of its occupants and their relationship to each other.

PAGE 75 Mai Mai faces the rising sun, which casts its city view into silhouette in the morning; during the evening the same view is bathed in a soft glow. **PREVIOUS SPREAD** Mai Mai's street façade is carved into a pattern of feathers. The electrically operated front door, at nearly 600 millimetres (24 inches) thick, closes invisibly as a secret panel flush within it. **OPPOSITE** The home is situated in the city's restaurant precinct and at night its white carved feather façade is illuminated by projections telling the story of its occupants. New Zealand fauna had no evolutionary native land mammal species – it was the land of birds.

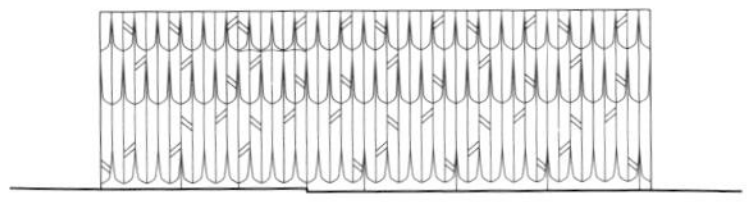

WEST ELEVATION

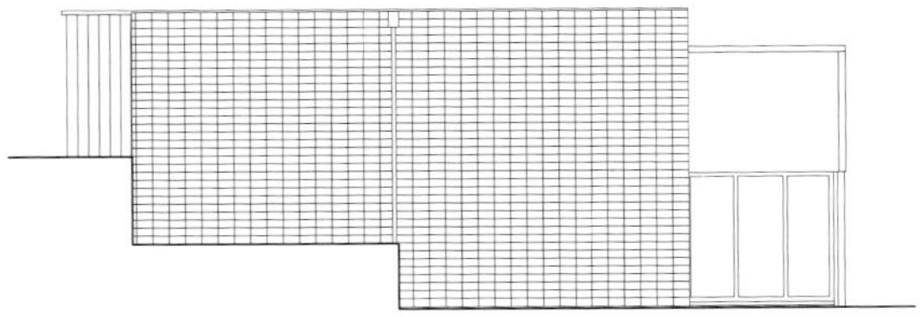

SOUTH ELEVATION

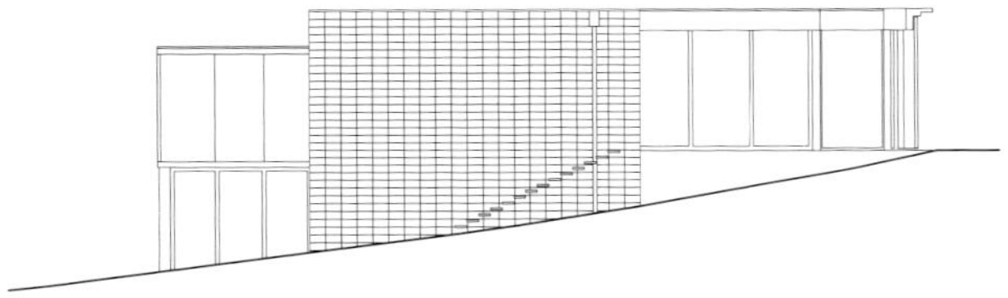

NORTH ELEVATION

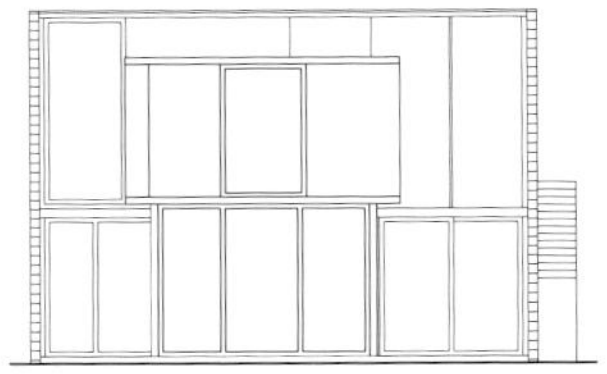

EAST ELEVATION

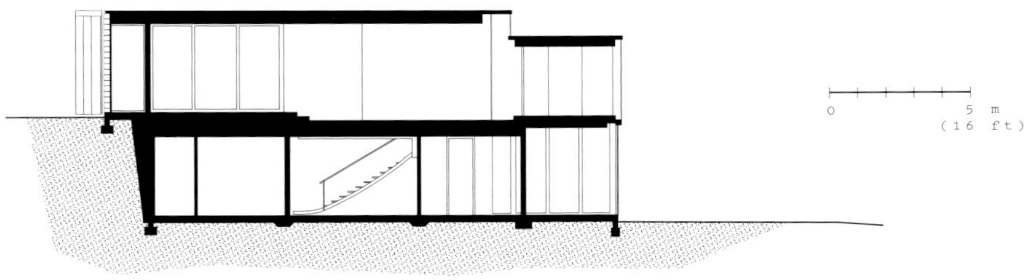

CROSS SECTION

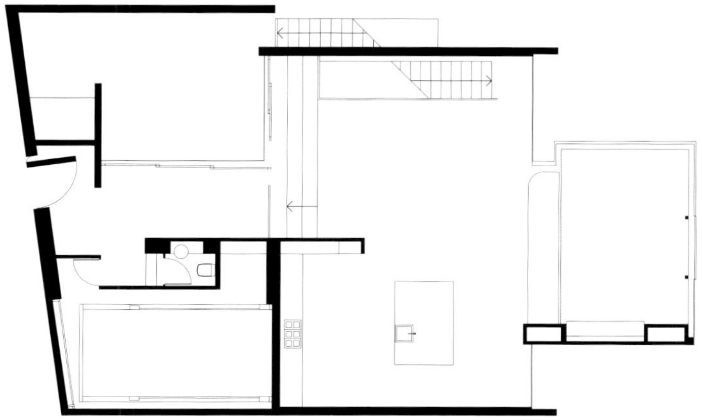

UPPER FLOOR PLAN

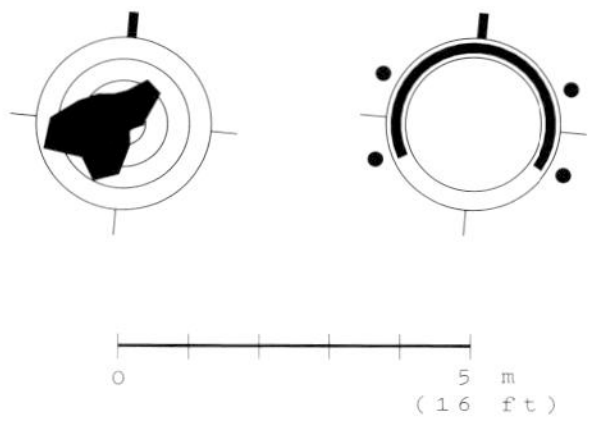

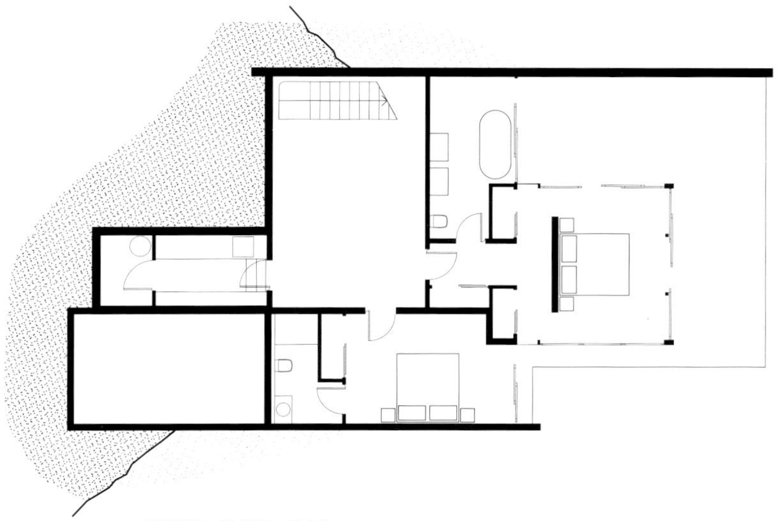

GROUND FLOOR PLAN

PREVIOUS SPREAD The third wall of the cantilevered glass cube is a mirrored fireplace. The floor is polished concrete. **OPPOSITE AND ABOVE** The walls of the upper floor are designed for the owners' collection of contemporary New Zealand art. A glass wall doubles the view as you enter.

OPPOSITE Mai Mai's subterranean 'nest' is a media room where the walls are clad in leather hides. A birdcage-like stair climbs to the viewing floor above. **ABOVE** Mai Mai faces the rising sun.

vero

PREVIOUS SPREAD The sitting room has the feel of a stage set where the actors are in dialogue with the life of the city. **ABOVE** Feathers of New Zealand native birds are projected onto Mai Mai's street façade, with its secret garage door that opens to a car stacker housing two cars. **OPPOSITE** Nighttime transforms the glass cube sitting room into an urban space floating in city lights.

LOCAL ROCK HOUSE

WAIHEKE / 2010

Waiheke Island is in New Zealand's Hauraki Gulf, around an hour by ferry from downtown Auckland City. This summer house sits on a steep coastal escarpment on Waiheke's northeastern coast. Access is via a single gravelled beach lane below.

The island is famous for its fine vineyards. Illustrious wines such as Cable Bay, Man o' War and Passage Rock are made possible by a rare geology. Beneath the many vineyards, seams of pyrite rock crisscross the land like veins, giving the grapes (mainly Cabernet Sauvignon, Malbec and Merlot) a distinctive local identity.

A home can bring a whole family together with a sense of place, each individual enjoying his or her own sense of belonging. A home is where memories are collected and stored.

This project is for an expatriate family who wanted a home here not only to re-establish but also to celebrate their New Zealand roots. It is built from the same local pyrite that gives belonging to Waiheke's wines. This is a dense, colourful, hard stone and as it ages it leaches vivid minerals, acquiring a rich texture. Until recently, pyrite was quarried primarily for use on the metal roads that wind their way over the island, but here it is stacked as a series of terraces in the escarpment. Each layer of the house provides views of the beach and off to the horizon.

The home's main living area is tucked safely into the escarpment between a seafront pool terrace and a western grotto-like courtyard that is often used as an outdoor movie theatre by the family. Above this, bedrooms are grouped at different levels: each is a finely scaled romantic louvred lookout in the canopy line of the trees that separate the beach from the hills. Every room is a private retreat in its own right and accessed by an individual stair. The automated bronze louvres control sunlight and provide visual shelter from the sometimes busy beach below.

The home is ecologically efficient. It uses an innovative passive air heating and cooling system by using the rock reservoir as a heat sink to provide even temperatures throughout the year. It has a large rainwater storage facility as well as on-site waste treatment and a reticulated water system.

Our hope is that by using the rock that belongs so clearly in this place the house will offer the occupants the very same sense of belonging here as memories begin to form and fill the home.

PREVIOUS SPREAD Waiheke's roads are gravelled in a local pyrite stone that also forms the gravelled soil type under the island's famous vineyards, giving the wine its distinctive terroir. Local Rock explores the use of the same stone to create a sense of local identity for its owners. **OPPOSITE** The pyrite rock ages wonderfully, increasing in patina with the passing of time. Here it has been used with chocolate-coloured aluminium blackout louvres, which close electronically at the flick of a switch. The home's lee courtyard can be glimpsed at the back.

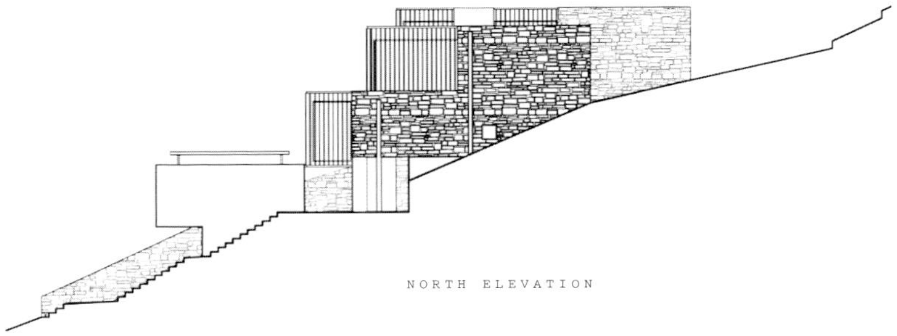

NORTH ELEVATION

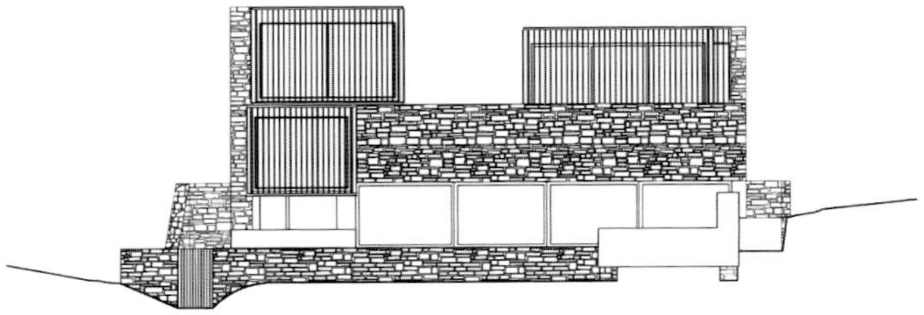

EAST ELEVATION

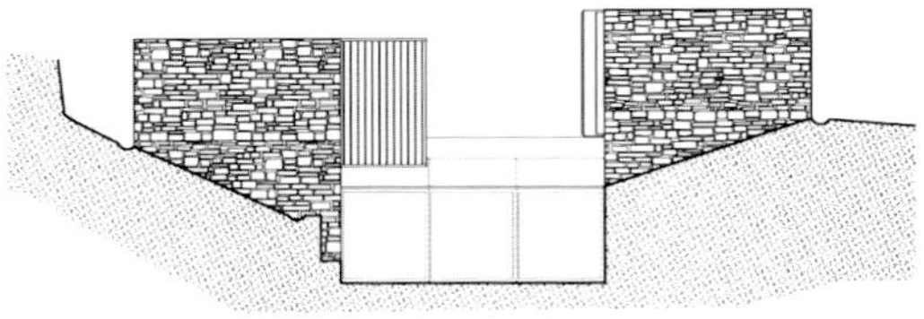

WEST ELEVATION

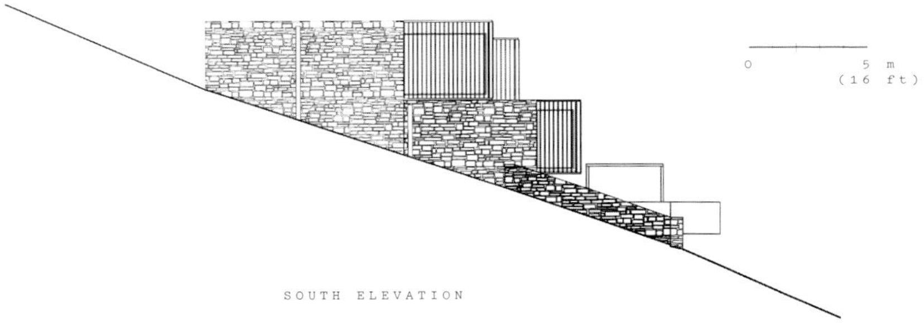

SOUTH ELEVATION

PREVIOUS SPREAD The home's main living floor sits under a rock bridge open to the beach views, with a protected split-level courtyard behind. Everything you need for a relaxing day is at hand in one simple open plan.

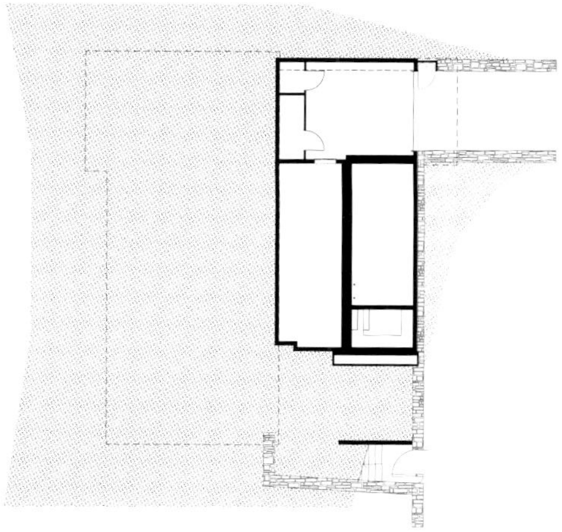

ENTRY LEVEL PLAN

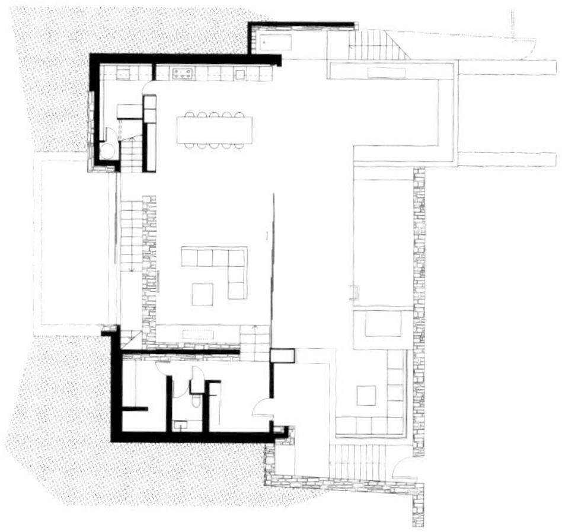

GROUND FLOOR PLAN

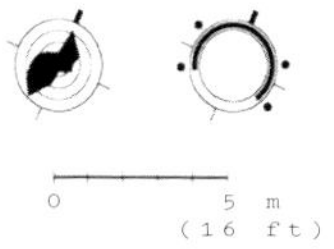

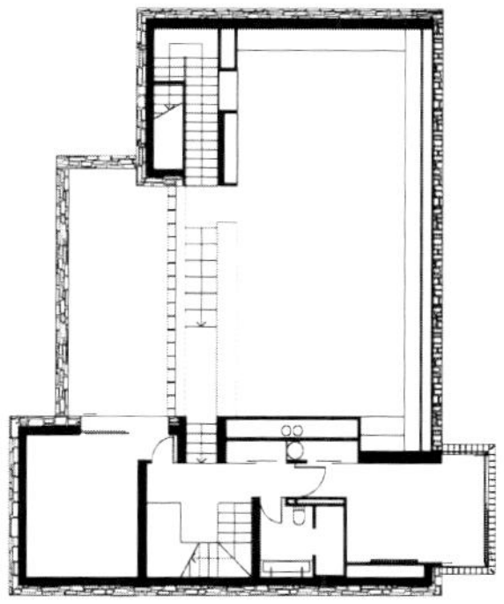

FIRST FLOOR PLAN

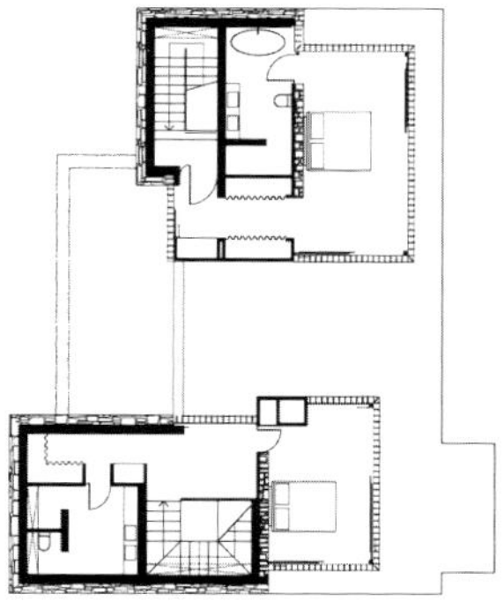

SECOND FLOOR PLAN

ABOVE The home is entered from a beach lane below. **OPPOSITE** Its gas fireplace is complemented by colour-stabilized timber veneers and chocolate-coloured aluminium cassette panels.

Each bedroom is located at the top of its own separate staircase and overlooks the beach below through automatic exterior blackout louvres.

PREVIOUS SPREAD Indoor/outdoor living is all on one big indoor/outdoor terrace above the beach. The guest 'cottage' is located on the roof level at left; the owner's suite is on the right. **ABOVE AND OPPOSITE** A large sculpture occupies the roof space between the owners' suite and the guest cottage. Lazy days in the sun end in still nights and the sound of the waves lapping on the white sand below.

ST STEPHEN'S

AUCKLAND / 2014

Sonja and Glenn are wonderful supporters of our work. This is their family home and sits in a stately street lined with plane trees.

Living happily just a few doors up the street in the house where they had raised their four children, when this property came on to the market they saw it as an opportunity to refine their ideas on how they wanted to live. Here, they can provide for the frequent return visits of their now university-aged children, often with friends in tow. With family, gardening and cooking central to their lives, the possibility of a bigger outdoor area also greatly appealed.

While Sonja and Glenn held strong views on how they wanted to live in their home, they were very open to the creative process. Their only two non-negotiables: that the home be full of light and sun, and that it be strongly connected to the land. With this in mind we set about creating a pavilion in a garden – a country house in an urban setting.

The design is inspired by the symmetry of late-1960s Italian modernist buildings. For the exterior, we created a pattern from alternating windows and glass-reinforced-concrete panels within a steel-framed structure. The front of the house is open and informal in comparison to the high fences and security gates of neighbouring properties – this suits the owners' open way of life.

A formal motor court is flanked on either side by green-roof garages, and the street-facing walls of the garages continue to soften as their ficus cover spreads, a clue to the thriving gardens found behind them. The gently sloping site gave us the opportunity to step the living areas down below entrance level, allowing the home's volume to open up to an unexpected 3.8 metre-high (12½ foot) ceiling.

Early on in the process we had discussed the indefinable qualities of new and old in existing homes and the interesting juxtapositions that are often lacking in contemporary home design. This discussion translated into the challenge of creating a brand new home that possesses a personality that is timeless, light-filled and classic, but with an obvious soul.

PREVIOUS SPREAD The home is symmetrical on all four sides and sits on a leafy plane-tree-lined avenue. The motor court sits slightly below the level of the road. The ficus will grow to cover the garages and gym flanking the motor court. **OPPOSITE** The structure of St Stephen's is formed from a steel scaffold painted in micaceous iron oxide and hung with panels of concrete that form a geometric pattern of alternating balconies. The window joinery is steel as well.

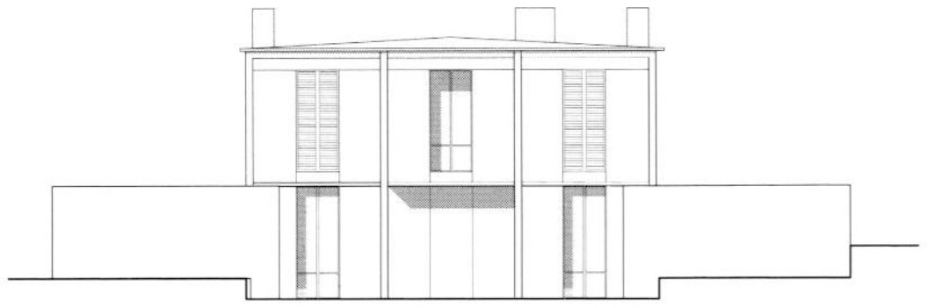

EAST ELEVATION

NORTH ELEVATION

SOUTH ELEVATION

WEST ELEVATION

0 5 m
(16 ft)

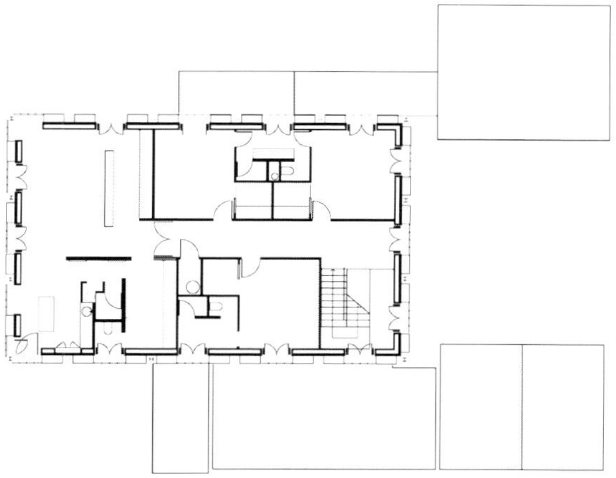

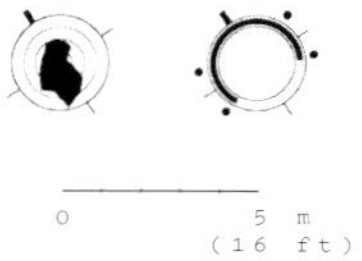

UPPER LEVEL PLAN

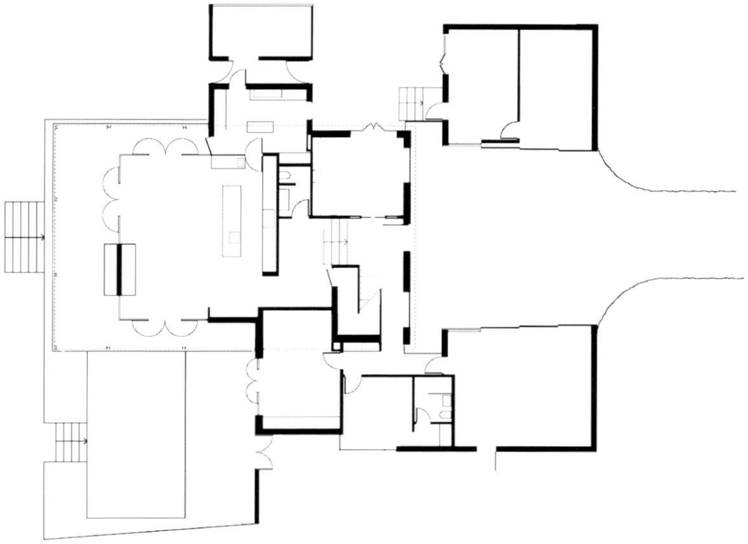

GROUND FLOOR PLAN

The main living room has a 3.8 metre-high (12½ foot) ceiling and has a blackened steel fireplace as its focal point. The 'nursery plant' to the right of the fireplace is a bronze artwork by Michael Parekowhai.

Glenn and Sonja's suite acts as an open-plan studio for their sumptuous art collection. From here they have views of the city and harbour.

An eclectic kitchen, developed in collaboration with Sonja, an interior designer, is the centre of family life. The butler's pantry, separated by the glass wall on the left, is part of the garden's circulation and doubles as a gardening workroom.

OPPOSITE, ABOVE AND OVERLEAF St Stephen's sits in the middle of a rectangular garden planted mainly in flowers and edibles. Conceptually it is a 'farmhouse in the city'. Life here is about family, friends and food. The exterior is symmetrical on all four elevations.

THINKING IN PATTERNS

Mā mua ka tika a muri.

The past, present and future are one space we are walking through.

Polynesian language is an oral rather than a written tradition. Pattern and memory play a key part in storytelling and passing knowledge on through the generations.

In Māori architecture the *wharenui*, or meeting house, is a pattern of the people who use the building. Just as elements of the environment such as lakes, rivers and mountains are identities in their own right with human characteristics, so too is the *wharenui*.

The *wharenui* forms the most fundamental private realm and unity of Māori society. Its form and structure resemble a body, arms stretched out ready to embrace; the face and spine of the founding ancestor is at the ridge, while rafters as the ribs are supported by carved panels representing ancestors of the people the building has been designed for.

The people belong to the *wharenui*, the *wharenui* belongs to them. The building

is a pattern or model for life and relationships.

Rather than the Western architectural concept where the focus is on space, light and materials, in the Māori way of thinking, form follows whānau, the extended family for whom the building is intended.

ABOVE Meeting house interior at Muriwai, Gisborne

NORTHLAND FARMHOUSE

KERIKERI / 2017

This house is for an overseas family. They had a very clear vision for the home, with a detailed brief on both its form and its function. Their days here are about farming, fishing, diving and walking the land with friends and family. They wanted the setting up and shutting down of the house to be fast and effortless.

The 550-square-metre (6,000-square-foot) home is on a 2,000-hectare (5,000-acre) sheep and cattle station that occupies one side of a peninsula in the subtropical far north of Te Ika-a-Māui, New Zealand's North Island. The station is a dry stock (pasture grazing) coastal escarpment sloping directly in to the afternoon sun. A pool house, the pool and the main building are situated to command wide views across the farm and out over the sea to the horizon – a view that would be uninterrupted were it not for the Cavalli Islands floating majestically centre-stage a few kilometres out into the Pacific.

The project is an exploration of ethereal classical traditions of 'a place to contain a conciousness', in this case a family. It is clad simply – a vertically running knotted red cedar exterior lined in local macrocarpa, all hung on twin two-way longitudinal trusses. The truss supports allow the exterior walls of the building to slide away or be closed quickly depending on occupancy or weather. This transforms what seems at first glance to be a utilitarian farm shed into an open, airy pavilion.

The garden is natural and maintenance-free, containing as it does only plants native to the peninsula. The thermal core of the building is constructed from volcanic rock sourced from the immediate area. Local stone also provided material for the basalt bath and 25 metre (82 foot) saltwater infinity pool.

The home's exterior sliding skin is designed to weather. In between visits it blends in like a farm building, while the interior remains eternal – unchanging through the seasons, consistent year after year, visit after visit.

PAGE 127 The setting for the Northland Farmhouse. **PREVIOUS SPREAD** The Northland Farmhouse shuts down when its owners are away, with huge macrocarpa-clad sliding walls. This makes the interior infinitely adjustable and the home's connection to the landscape dynamic. **OPPOSITE** These buildings are designed to look like utility buildings on the farm when unoccupied. A long stone infinity pool runs from the games pavilion out to the view.

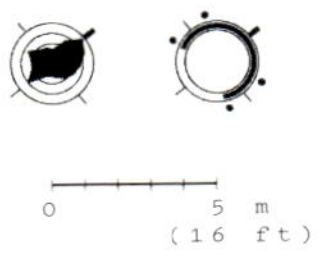

UPPER LEVEL PLAN

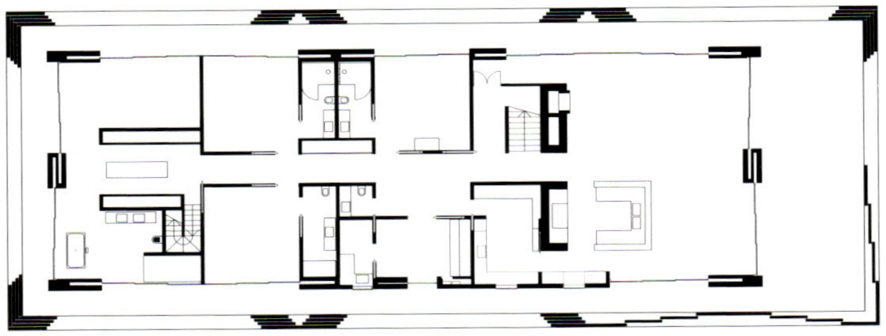

GROUND FLOOR PLAN

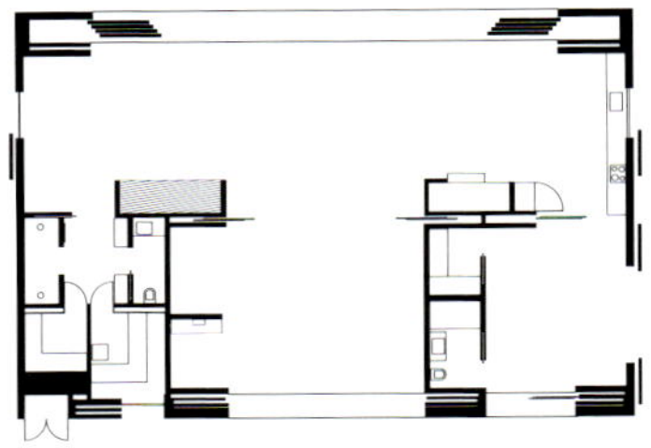

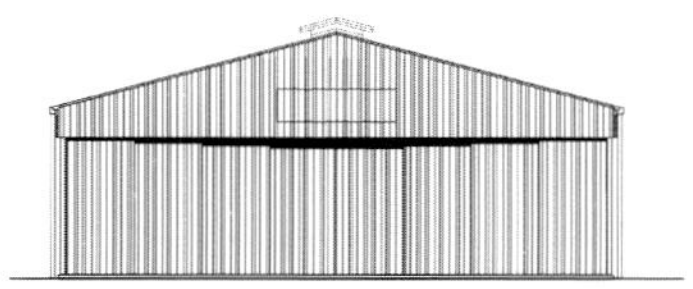

SOUTHWEST ELEVATION

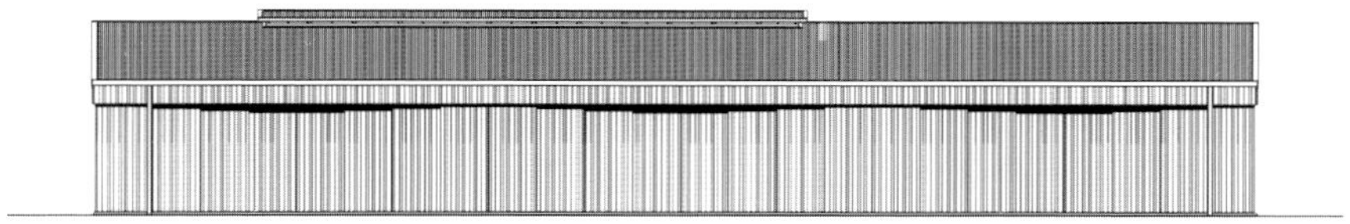

SOUTHEAST ELEVATION

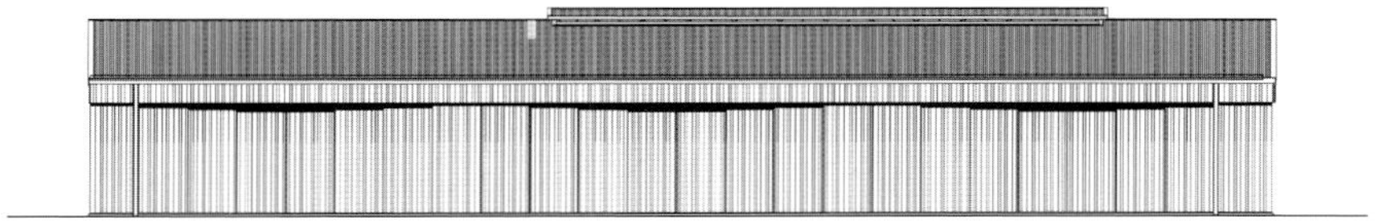

NORTHWEST ELEVATION

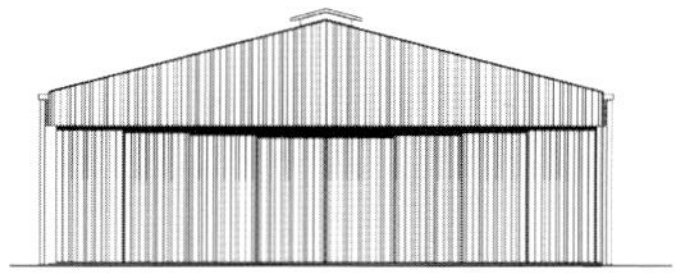

NORTHEAST ELEVATION

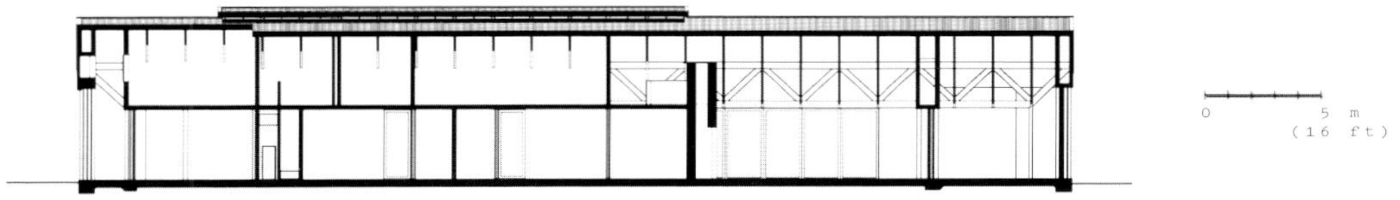

CROSS SECTION

The home's interior is constructed and lined in warm macrocarpa timber supported on large barn trusses with fittings and fixtures in black. The simplicity of the detailing disguises the hard work that has gone into it.

OPPOSITE Two matching warm central cores are constructed from stone quarried on the farm. They contain the fireplace, Aga stove and services. **ABOVE** The office upstairs has views to the outside through the building's outer skin.

OPPOSITE The outer walls slide away or close completely. This enables the outdoor furniture to be left in place when unused and the whole building can be secured quickly and opened again just as easily. The view from the games room opens out as the house is opened up. **ABOVE** The basalt pool is a four-sided infinity pool.

The home's sliding outer walls are hung on twin glulam (glued laminated timber) trusses that run the full length of the house; all the outer walls slide into just five stacks. Inside and outside living remains unchanged and protected from year to year.

KINLOCH

LAKE TAUPO / 2016

Kinloch lodge overlooks Lake Taupo on New Zealand's high volcanic plateau.

The golf course has a rolling highland feel, with rugged surroundings including mountainous tundra. The lodge stands above the golf course, dominating from a windswept rocky escarpment.

It is constructed in bagged stone on blockwork and is punctuated by turret-like chimneys. There is juxtaposition within the structure, which is strong, resilient and pragmatic, but at the same time romantic.

Rather than assembling spaces with an arrangement of floor, walls and roof, the interior of the lodge has been designed as if hollowed out from a single rock form.

Very high portrait windows frame the volcanic plateau in the distance. As if looking through binoculars, the view is brought in very close.

The wind here is bitter and constant. This is where the centre of the North Island rises sharply into a more hostile environment. Gone are the rolling green hills. Facing southward across the deep blue lake to distant snow-capped volcanoes, the building wraps defensively around itself, forming protected, sunny courtyards and battlement-type walks.

PREVIOUS SPREAD Kinloch lodge stands sentinel facing into the prevailing wind on a rocky escarpment looking out to New Zealand's volcanic central plateau. **OPPOSITE** Access to the lodge is through a landscape of volcanic grass, often covered in wild flowers.

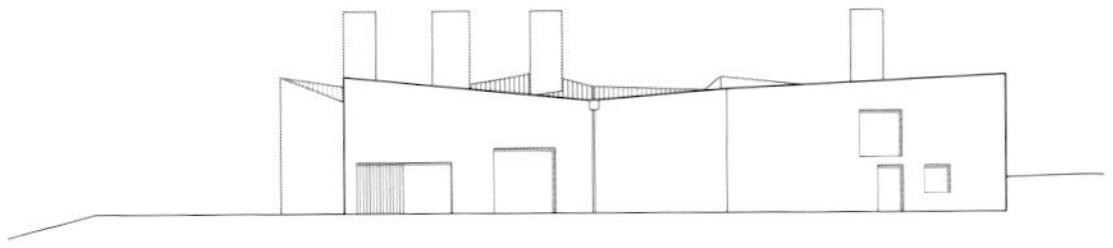

EAST ELEVATION

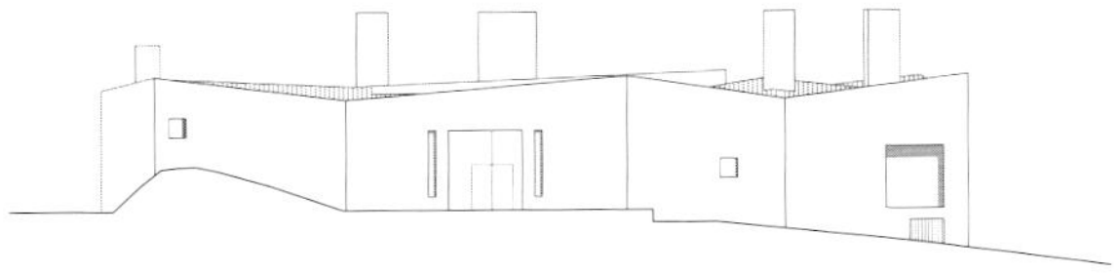

NORTH ELEVATION

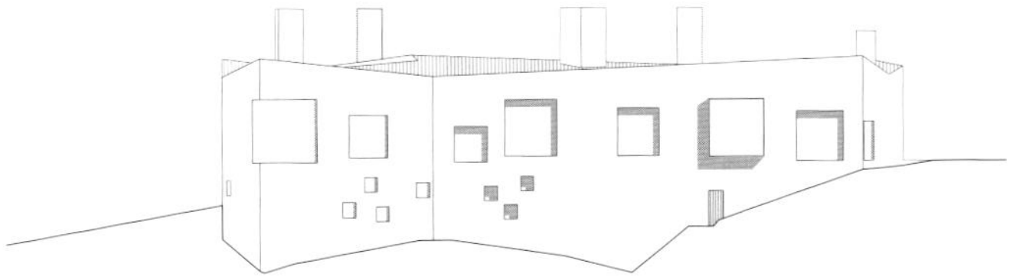

SOUTH ELEVATION

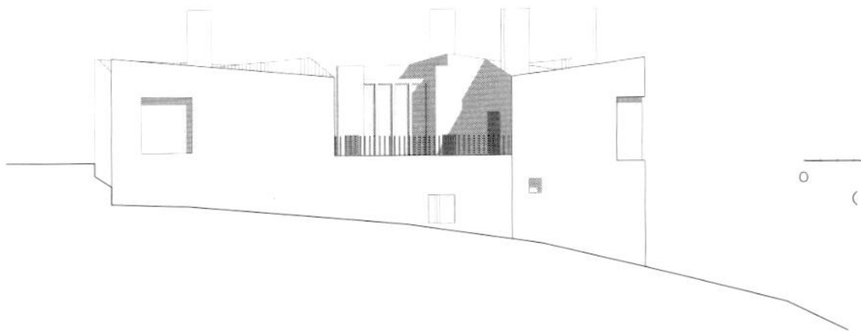

0 5 m
(16 ft)

WEST ELEVATION

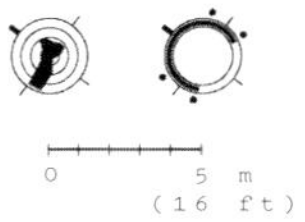

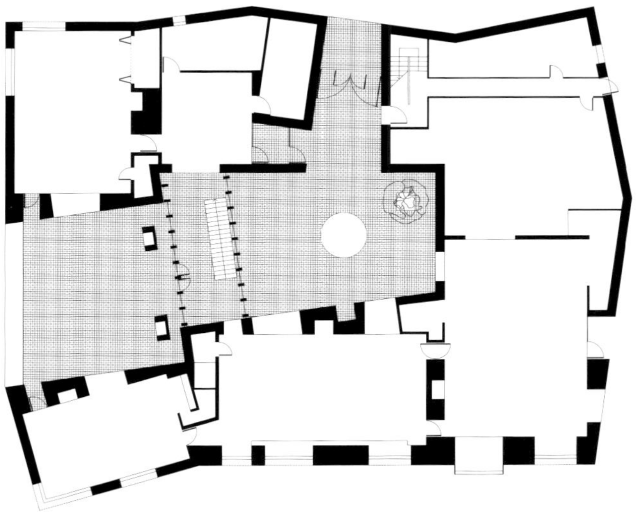

GROUND FLOOR PLAN

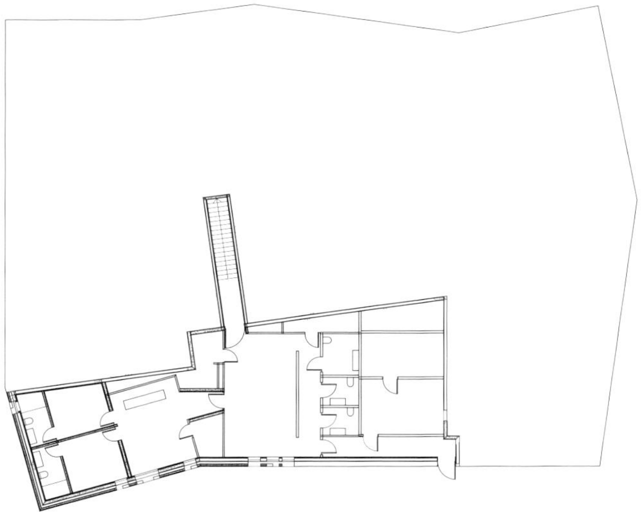

BASEMENT PLAN

A double-sided, glazed cloister that bisects the lodge's central courtyard gives access to its main reception rooms. Recreation areas and the wine cellar are underneath.

ABOVE Mountain and lake views are brought deep into the lodge through framed apertures acting telescopically. **OPPOSITE** The lodge's great room has two matching and flanking fireplaces, and is walled in plastered stone. Conceptually, we designed the spaces as if hollowing them out from a single masonry block rather than assembling them out of walls and ceilings.

The dining room can be subdivided into private dining areas by means of curtains.

A central courtyard provides outdoor space sheltered from the prevailing wind and also doubles as the lodge's reception area. In its centre is a water mirror made from a Corten steel disc set flush with the cobbles: when the fire is alight, the flames of the welcoming hearth are reflected in this. The single oak tree will grow and spread to cover one third of the courtyard.

The lodge's outer walls are patterned in bagged rock punctuated by viewing windows, some monumental in scale. All are in the same 1:1.3 proportion. Turret-like chimneys top the building.

THE MICHAEL HILL CLUBHOUSE

QUEENSTOWN / 2008

Hunkered down into the earth so as not to bother the landscape above, this is a private *wharenui* for a jeweller who is also a golfer. Its design seeks to integrate the identity of its owner into the experience of the landscape and in so doing intensify that identity. It is generated primarily around the game of golf and its own relationship with the terrain.

The clubhouse sits in the Wakatipu Basin, deep in the Southern Alps of New Zealand.

The Remarkables mountain range is clearly visible from the site, and taking this as a cue the building responds to the exciting topography that surrounds it.

Sir Michael wanted a place that could serve as a 'private box' and then convert to a gateway for corporate events. All of the rooms are set around a fireside courtyard, and the external staircase emerges from the ground not only to create but to celebrate a gateway to the temporary tent village that is erected on the grounds during tournaments.

The building's plan is anthropomorphic around a central service spine: carts are located at the foot of the building, the restaurant at the head and spa rooms in the centre. In plan, section and elevation this design adheres to the geometry of interrelated skewed quadrilaterals. It is a pattern of Papatūānuku, the Earth Mother.

Large expanses of frameless glass invite the mountains outside to come in.

We wanted the form to appear to have evolved from the same forces that generated the land around it both geologically and metaphorically. The Earth Mother is represented by sensual curves and materials, while the splintering angles reflect the ongoing geological uplift that continues to form the mountains around it as they seek to push the sky away.

PREVIOUS SPREAD This clubhouse explores the New Zealand creation story of Rangi and Papa: the Earth Mother and the Sky Father prised apart by tectonic forces as a sculptural composition. Earthquakes are common in this part of New Zealand's Southern Alps and the building sits near a fault line known as 'the Great Divide'. **OPPOSITE** Two elevations of the clubhouse hunker down into the earth allowing the game of golf to be played around it (or on it!).

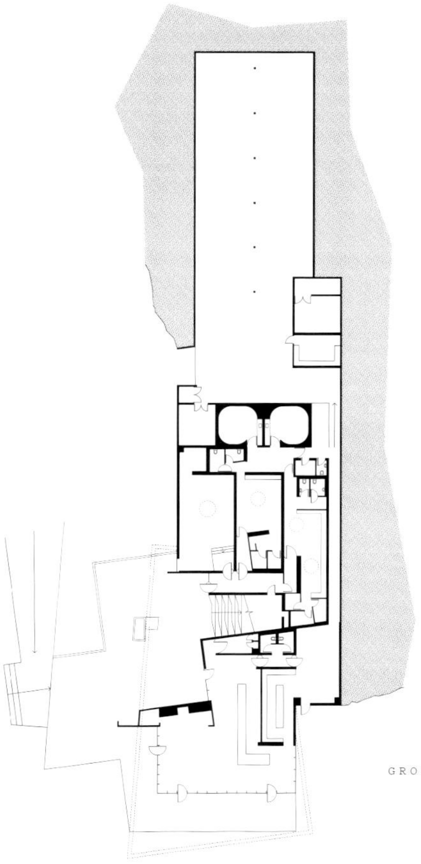

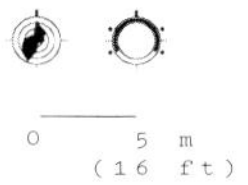

GROUND FLOOR PLAN

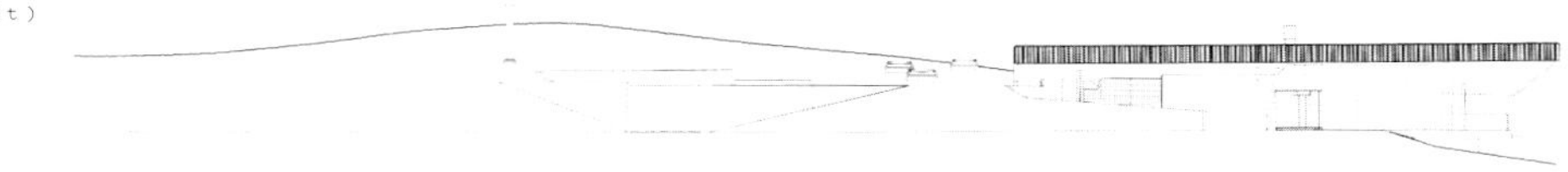

WEST ELEVATION

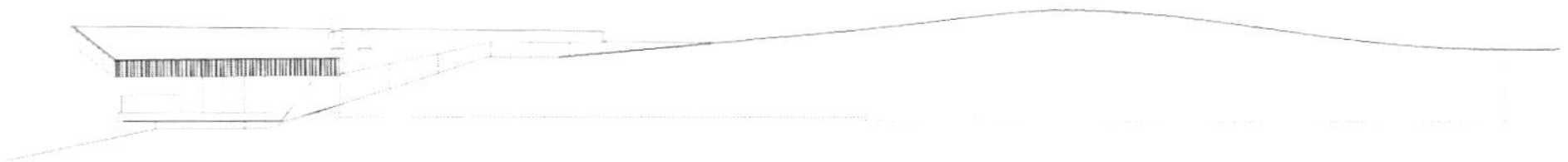

EAST ELEVATION

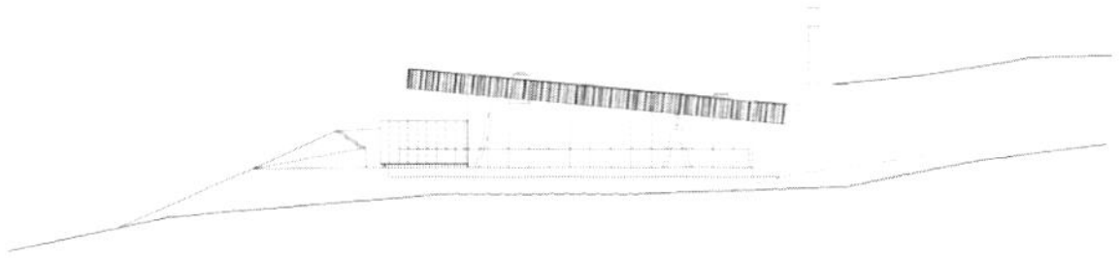

SOUTH ELEVATION

OPPOSITE This project is a 'private box' for an avid golfer who is also a jeweller. Here the view looking to the 18th green is shown. **FOLLOWING SPREAD** It is not unusual for members here to play golf off the roof during post-game drinks and dinner.

NAISOSO

FIJI / 2017

Our clients Raina and Tejash were living in Fiji with Tejash's parents and, although a very close family, they wanted a home of their own.

Both of their families had lived for generations in Fiji, but, like many, they had been educated and developed their successful careers overseas. They chose to come back to their homeland while maintaining an international outlook and sensibility. Fiji is perfectly located for such an ideal, centrally placed for the USA, Asia, Australia and New Zealand.

They came to us with a slice of an extraordinary tropical island paradise, the stuff of dreams – a rectangular, level plot of 3,000 square metres (32,000 square feet), facing the setting sun. On one side, you step directly onto a private crescent-shaped beach where the sand is as white as sugar and the view reaches across to the Mamanuca and Yasawa Island groups. On the other, land side, you look east over a tidal river winding towards a tropical mountain range known as the Sleeping Giant. Of particular delight for Tejash is the site's proximity to the airport.

Raina and Tejash wanted a large, secure home for children and for a very large family who could come to stay for long periods. They wanted their home to be 'Fijian', and also to be contemporary and of its age, to contribute to the increasingly hopeful Fiji that they represent internationally.

The concept of a clean white space opening to both sides was arrived at quite quickly, but the design kept growing as we started to realize just how many people this couple could gather around them. We devised a house with a simple in-situ poured-concrete structural frame and envelope. Onto this we bolted pre-made aluminium windows to grade 8 cyclone standard. These sit beneath aluminium security fins bolted in place to act as storm shutters and sun shades. A simple coral stone wall adds texture to an all-white interior on cool concrete floors set around the enormous L-shaped horizon pool. Deep in the house, in protected spaces, are all the electronics and services.

Building in Fiji comes with its challenges, not the least of them being 'Island time' – construction does not happen quickly and is subject to a handful of local peculiarities. Tolerances and materials have to be simple, construction has to be kept basic. Then there are the island's regular cyclones, tropical downpours and floods to deal with.

The construction process was testing. But with huge credit to the builder and the owners, we managed to stay true to the original vision.

PREVIOUS SPREAD This house consists of a beach pavilion and recreation room to the left with guest cottage on the right. The main reception rooms are in the middle and the owners' suite is upstairs. **OPPOSITE** The view from the main entry to the Mamanuca and Yasawa Islands over a raised infinity pool. The pool combines with the beach pavilion to form a T shape.

All exterior doors slide into recess pockets, completely transforming the interior to exterior, free of glass for most of the year. The beach-front pavilion includes a recreation room and an outdoor kitchen.

NORTH ELEVATION

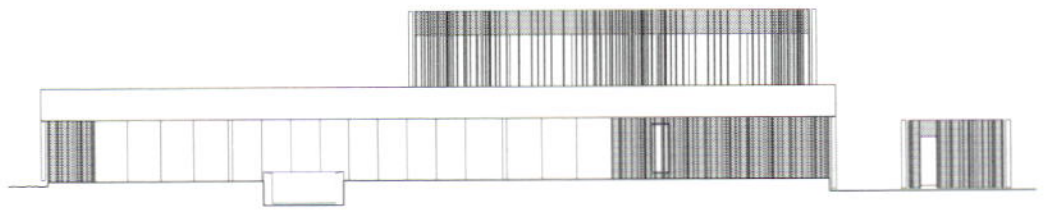

WEST ELEVATION

EAST ELEVATION

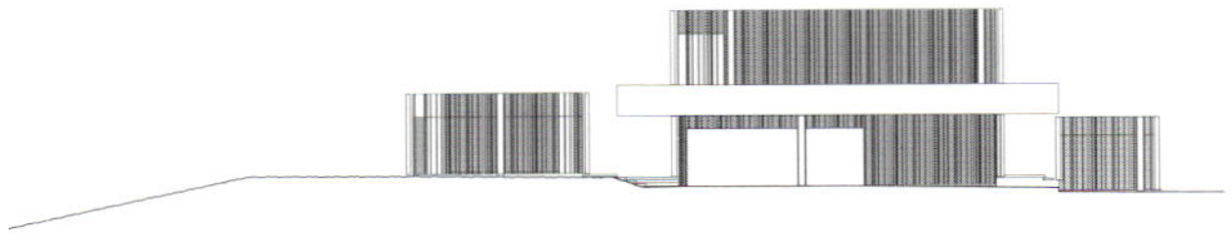

SOUTH ELEVATION

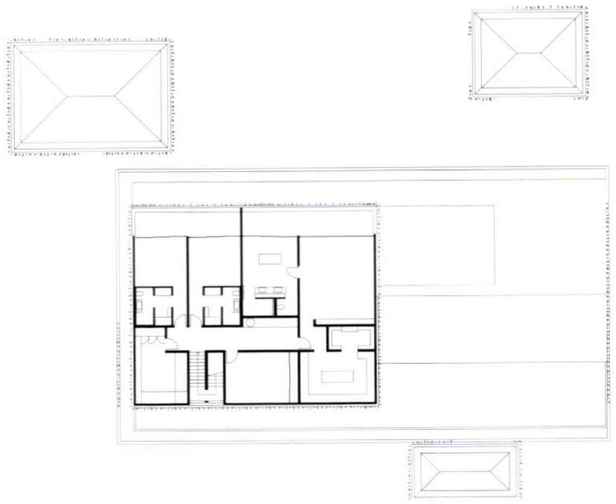

UPPER FLOOR PLAN

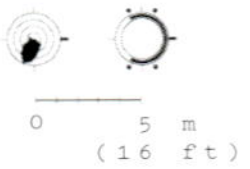

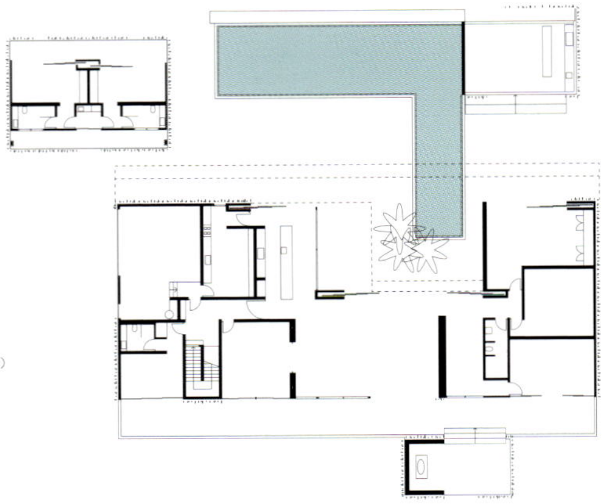

GROUND FLOOR PLAN

OPPOSITE AND OVERLEAF The house looks towards the sunset over a soft-white-sand beach. It uses aluminium cyclone shutters as its aesthetic; these are set on a simple poured-concrete shell painted white. The effect is almost curtain-like.

THE SEARCH FOR BEAUTY

'The object we love is uniquely beautiful,
but that beauty is not unique to the object,
rather, it is a universal beauty'

Plato, *Symposium* (c.385-370 BC)

One of the traditional goals of building is to create beauty. The emphasis on what is beautiful has shifted through the ages between proportion, moral and physical truths and the eye of the beholder.

What does this mean in today's world? What is beauty? Is it even important? Is being beautiful really a definitive test for good design?

New Zealand is one of a handful of countries on earth with beauty as a defining characteristic. Allow anyone just one adjective to describe New Zealand and they will almost certainly choose 'beautiful'. For us, our country provides an opportunity to understand what beauty actually is.

The Darwinian view of beauty suggests that it is an evolved survival mechanism. You know something is beautiful unconsciously in much the same way that the flight or fight response is unconscious. It is an instinct.

Nobel Prize-winning physicist Murray Gell-Mann observes that in the field of quantum physics, where empirical testing of particles is not possible, beauty is commonly the criterion for a successful theory: 'What is especially striking and remarkable is that in fundamental physics a beautiful or elegant theory is more likely to be right than a theory that is inelegant.' He describes the attributes of beauty as these: universal (for example, gravity applies as much to the moon as to Newton's apple); being the simplest expression possible; and having clarity and symmetry.

Our brain looks for simple patterns to recognize, and when it does, it is the familiarity or symmetry, or lack of it, that quickly tells us whether to admire or fear whatever it is that we are looking at.

Many ancient spiritual practices have held that the higher your level of consciousness, the greater level of beauty you can perceive. Today, this can be manipulated with mindfulness. Neurologists call this an upward spiral. It applies to beauty, together with other positive emotions, such as gratitude, trust, hope, truth and, of course, love.

When we look at it this way, beauty in architecture is like our environment giving us a warm hug.

If universal beauty is a sense of consciousness, maybe collective recognition of such beauty confirms the Darwinian hard-wired theory. Just as the proportions of the human body can elicit a sensual feeling, other qualities of human consciousness, such as honesty, truth, generosity and love, are recognized collectively as pattern models in our brain and generate a feeling of belonging. And when we belong, we easily recognize beauty. Recent phenomenology, the study of the structure of consciousness and experience, suggests that a building's beauty relates directly to the relationship it has with its physical and human environments – a relationship that starts with the architect and connects him or her eventually with the people for whom the building was intended.

THE PINES

MATARANGI / 2005

The coastline of New Zealand is a crown studded with jewels and everyone has their personal favourite.

All around the coast are communities of the summer houses known locally as baches. Some of these have simply sprouted from campsites and become groups of tiny ramshackle cottages huddled together. Baches can stay in families for generations. They are often erected quickly and intended only as temporary structures but then added to over the years. They are character-rich and crammed with memorabilia.

The bach is a tool for keeping families together, as succeeding generations spend their summer days fishing, cooking and playing cricket or touch rugby on the beach. These buildings are base camps from which the environment can be explored and enjoyed. In common they have the need to provide shelter in on-shore and off-shore winds, the need to be as maintenance-free as possible, and the need to be able to draw all sorts of different family life stages together at once. Children and teenagers can roam freely, never far from the sight of neighbouring friends, while adults can mix without the need to drive, all in a relaxed Arcadian environment where the door of every house is always open.

This particular bach is located on land previously used as a pine plantation fronting a white-sand surf beach called Matarangi. The remaining pines give a violet dappled light.

It consists of a main house, a sleep-out that acts as an outdoor entry lobby, and a boatshed with a two-bedroomed guest cottage above. The main house can be completely opened up along the front to a common reserve over a sociable, inviting deck. Its form is organized into two corrugated-zinc-clad volumes connected by a living space. The zinc cladding carries through to the interior, giving the effect that perhaps these were two separate, romantic structures joined later to become one.

Communal space continues to the protected courtyard area at the back with its external stone fireplace. This is the lee side of the building, through which the other buildings are accessed. Everything is positioned to afford glimpses of the ocean; every room has a different quality and relationship with the rest of the building. There is no front door.

The zinc ages gracefully so never needs to be painted. Inside, the walls are lined in painted larch and covered in local artwork, while furniture cast-offs litter the floor. Shutters on hydraulic stays close down windows, offering protection from the salt spray blown in from the beach out front. There are no downpipes, for they would only be blocked by pine needles. The bach remains constant from one summer to the next, waiting out the cooler months knowing that soon it will occupy its place at the centre of the family again.

PAGE 179 AND PREVIOUS SPREAD This house is constructed from solid corrugated gunmetal zinc. It was built in the early 1990s in an old *Pinus radiata* forestry plantation. **OPPOSITE** Every morning the home awakens to the sound of birdsong over rumbling surf. Each pavilion that makes up the house is a different room; some are connected to create larger spaces.

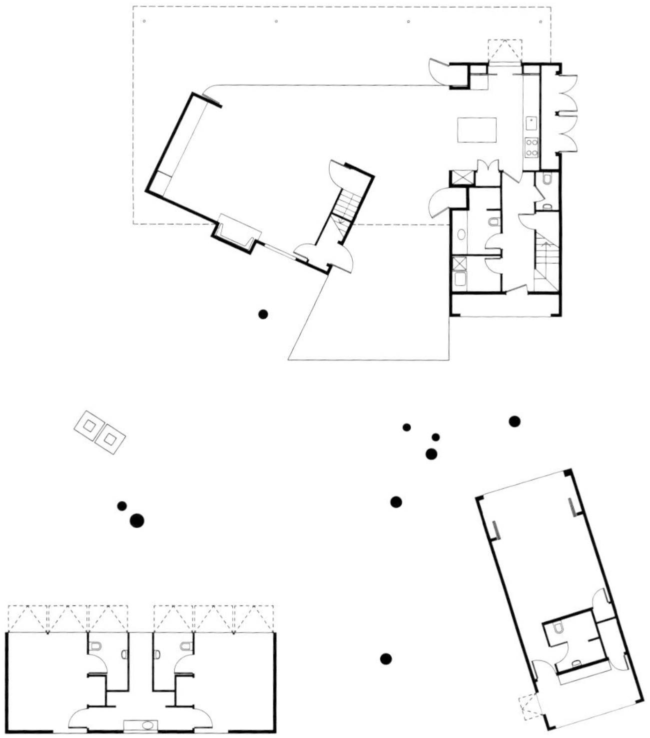

GROUND FLOOR PLAN

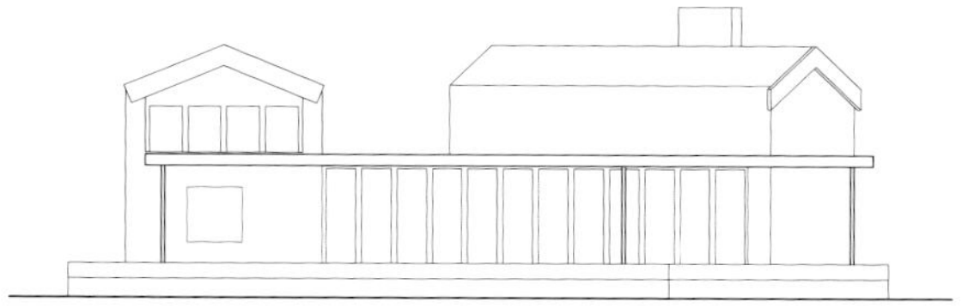

ELEVATION

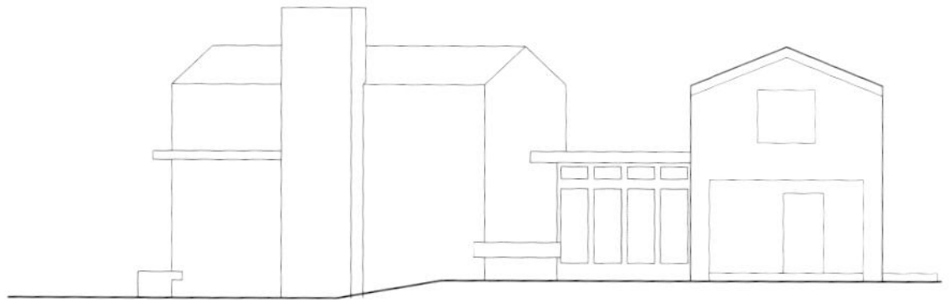

ELEVATION

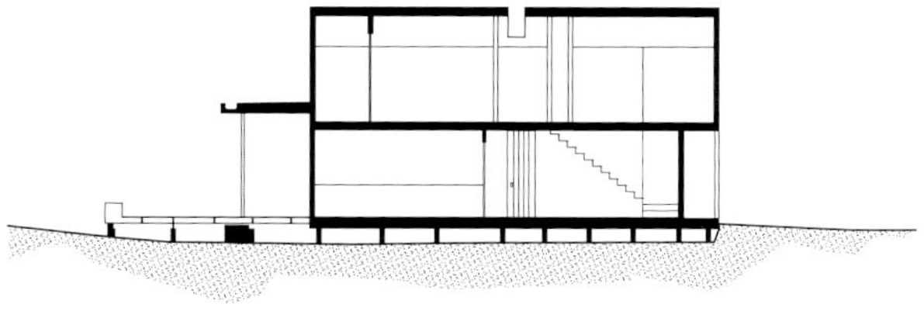

CROSS SECTION

OPPOSITE A long verandah runs parallel to the beach, and doors can be slid back into the walls during the summer months. In the evening the surrounding old forestry plantation is dappled in a violet and gold glow.

The home's outdoor living is created by the spaces between the buildings. There are four buildings in total: a living room with the master suite above; the kitchen and the children's bedrooms; a sleep-out backed by the property's outdoor entry lobby; and a two-bedroomed guest pavilion over the boatshed. There are no gutters on the roof so that the building can easily shed pine needles.

PREVIOUS SPREAD The old pine plantation fronts a white-sand surf beach just below the view. Balustrades form long daybeds. **OPPOSITE** The living building links through to the kitchen via an indoor/outdoor verandah that forms the main living space. The house is filled with Pacific memorabilia collected by the family. **ABOVE** A view of the property's wonderful white-sand surf beach.

M I L L B R O O K

ARROWTOWN / 2014

Millbrook is nestled just outside the small, picturebook-pretty heritage village of Arrowtown in New Zealand's Otago province, a former gold-mining town with numerous well-preserved buildings. The character of the home connects with the architecture in the local vernacular and the rural history of the region. Rather than just 'being there', it looks to celebrate and enrich that ongoing history. The home is a pattern of its built surroundings.

The typical architecture of old Otago includes smaller-scale buildings with thick schist walls, often plastered, and with deep recesses to vertically proportioned windows and door openings. This home continues this character in its form and materials.

Black aluminium doors and openings slide into the stone. The inside is top-lit, with warm natural light flooding in from the ceiling.

The home is a type of cruciform plan. Its interior is stained Oregon timber and exposed schist. Earthy tones bleed into the design of furniture and fittings.

The hope is that it will give its occupants a sense of belonging to the surrounding environment and community.

PREVIOUS SPREAD Millbrook House has a series of single plate-glass doors that slide completely into double-thickness schist walls. Twin fireplaces flank a central loggia under electronic louvres, allowing outdoor living even when it is cold and snowy. **OPPOSITE** Arrowtown, where the house is located, is a historic gold-mining village set deep into an alpine valley on New Zealand's Southern Alps. There is skiing, golf and jet boating nearby.

NORTHWEST ELEVATION

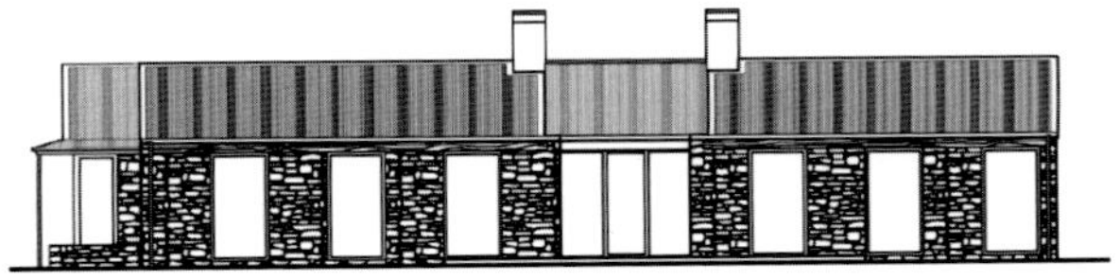

NORTHEAST ELEVATION

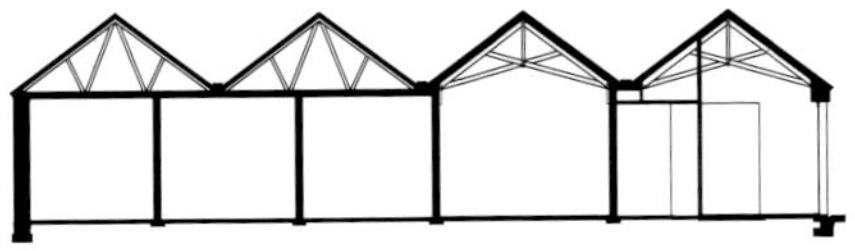

CROSS SECTION

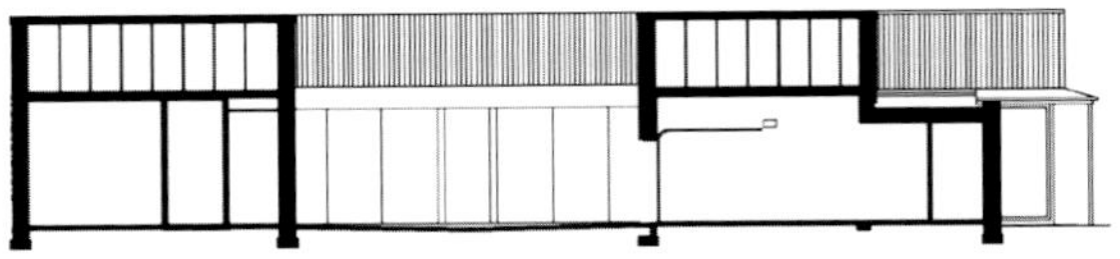

CROSS SECTION

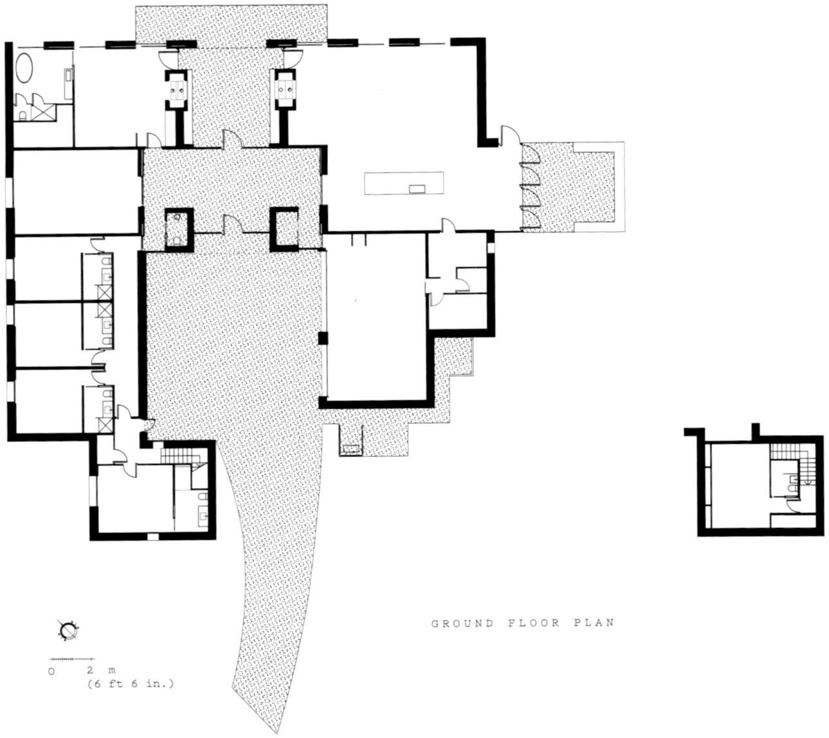

GROUND FLOOR PLAN

OPPOSITE There is a beautiful vista up to the area's main ski field, seen here in autumn. Outdoor zones are paved in the same local schist stone as the house.

The plan of the house is laid out in two halves around a double-fireplaced loggia backed by the home's entry lobby. All lighting, except feature lighting, is architecturally recessed.

ABOVE AND OPPOSITE In summer and autumn the spaces blend effortlessly from inside out into the bright alpine light. **FOLLOWING SPREAD** Seen in early autumn from below, the sculptural form of the home is reminiscent of a series of stacked gold-mining cottages.

WAIHEKE

WAIHEKE / 2017

This project is intended to be approached mainly by air – by helicopter, or even perhaps, one day, autonomous electric jet.

It is located on Waiheke Island and created for a family of adults who wish to participate in city life, but from a distance. This family wish to live together, but independently, with two houses operating as one.

It sits on a 4-hectare (10-acre) waterfront site facing west and is designed in response to an enormous 240-degree sea and island view. Acknowledging this, the plan is arranged around a trio of outdoor spaces, with two courtyards and a coastal terrace where shelter and view combinations can be found in any wind.

The building's simple form is a cedar-clad, monolithic timber slab or box hovering above the living and entertaining areas below. Inside it is the home's entry lobby from the landing pad above.

Services are contained in the wooden slab, and a series of large, deeply recessed rectangular skylights provide light, without direct sun, to the spaces below. The box works with the home's subterranean service areas, which are located beneath the helicopter pad.

PREVIOUS SPREAD This island home is designed to be accessed mainly by helicopter: the landing pad leads to the home's front door. The roof of the house is its principal façade and is expressed in a wood-grain pattern. **OPPOSITE** The home's bulk is divided into two parts: one underground and the other sheltering below a thick roof designed to modulate the strong New Zealand sunlight penetrating into the interior.

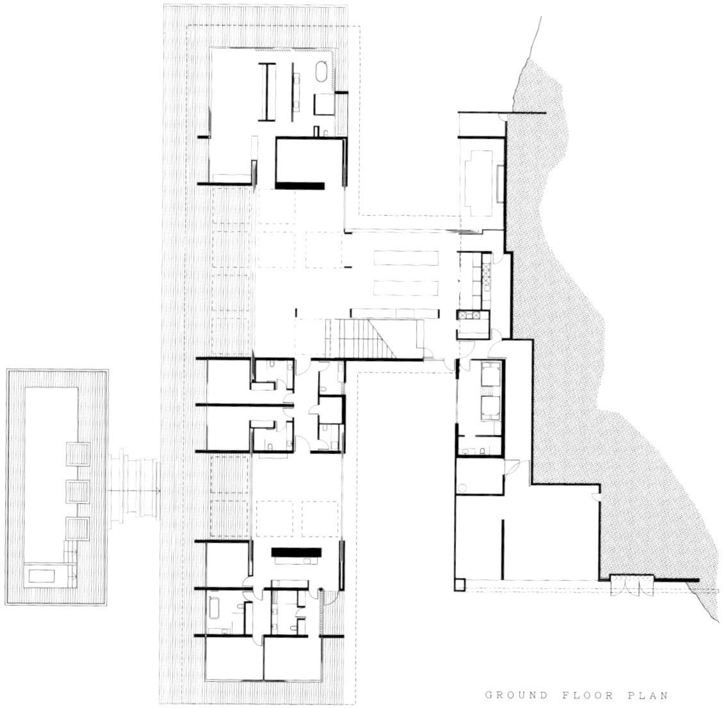

GROUND FLOOR PLAN

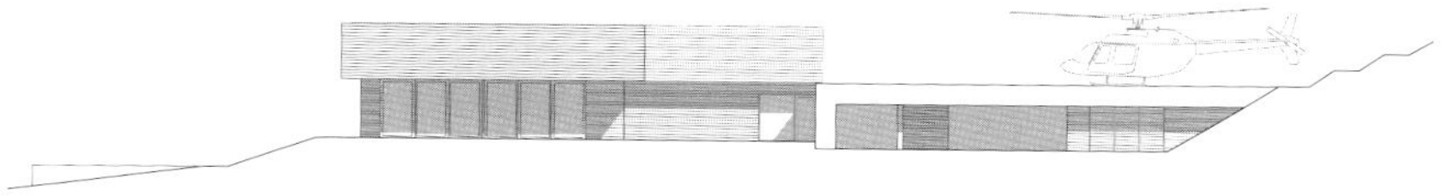

SOUTH ELEVATION

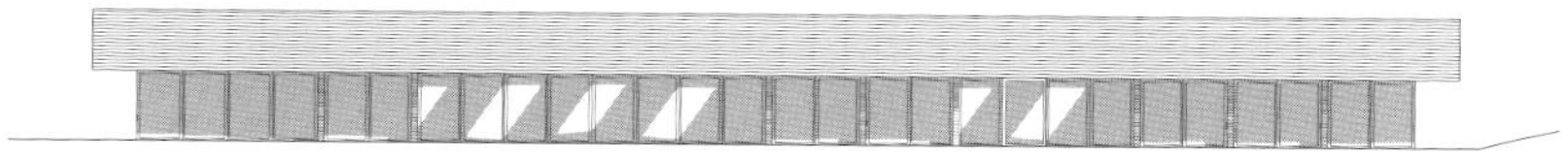

WEST ELEVATION

OPPOSITE At night the main entry stair down from the helicopter pad is lit with 870 flickering LED lights, just discernible in this daylight shot.

ABOVE, OPPOSITE AND FOLLOWING SPREAD The home enjoys a panoramic view of New Zealand's inner Hauraki Gulf and islands. The horizontality of the view informs the horizontality of the house. In its double-sided main living room, glass walls slide back into hidden pockets. The same timber boarding used to clad the house inside and out was also used for the shuttering and moulds for the concrete work. This makes all the exteriors and interiors one seamless pattern.

This outdoor room is the perfect place to listen to music with a glass of wine conveniently located on a shelf behind you. The thickness of the home's roof allows the interior volume to open up to unexpected heights, including to the helicopter pad above.

The plan of the house is actually two connected homes, one for parents and one for children, with two shared guest bedrooms accessing both. The children's end enjoys the swimming pool.

P A R I H O A

MURIWAI / 2009

Located on Auckland's rugged and stormy western coast, this home is the owners' facility for a large sheep and cattle station. The project explores the architectural typology of a fort or outpost, a form that is at once commanding and defensive.

Sixty metres (200 feet) below, wind and ocean crash to shore from the Tasman Sea. The shape of the building wraps around itself to offer protection from an unforgiving, exposed environment. There is no modification to the landscape, other than the sentry form of the building itself.

Simple strategies of converging and expanding walls create various spatial experiences. The entry lobby is guarded by a gate, keeping the sheep out, and sectioned perimeter walls pivot open to offer an unexpected link.

Long views reach uninterrupted to the sunset. Towards the edges of the structure, ocean, sky and hills open above, below, all around, until the immense grandeur of the environment is fully revealed simply as part of the experience of day-to-day living.

PREVIOUS SPREAD This farmhouse is for a 5,000-hectare (12,350-acre) sheep and cattle farm located on New Zealand's exposed West Coast. There is no garden; instead the house floor is raised and animals can roam freely around its perimeter. **OPPOSITE** The site is exposed to incredible still, clear days and beautiful sunsets as well as to howling Tasman Sea storms.

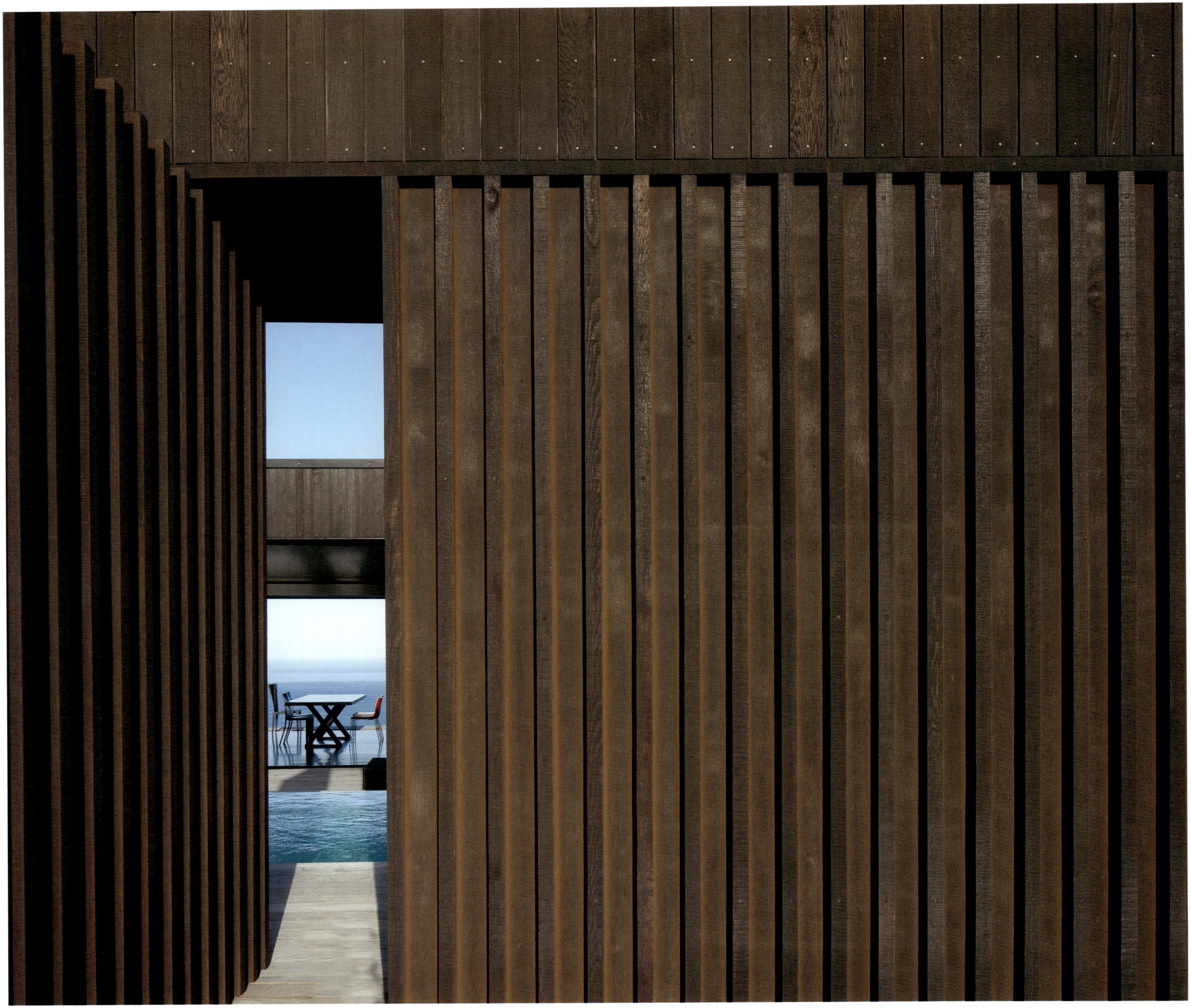

GROUND FLOOR PLAN

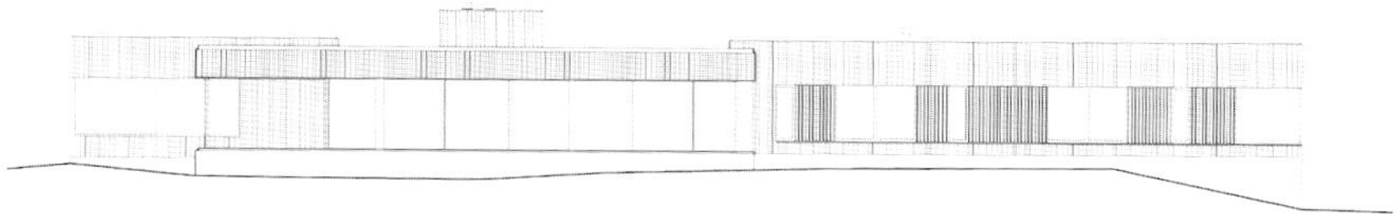

WEST ELEVATION

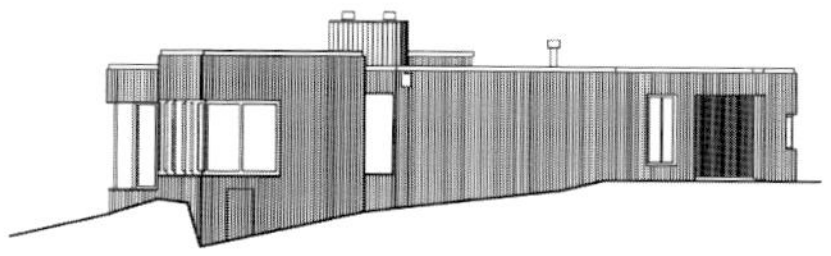

SOUTH ELEVATION

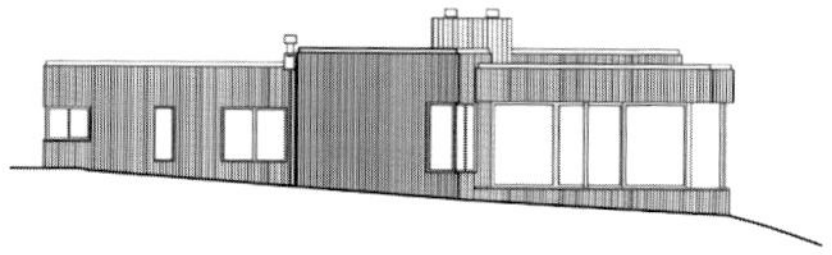

NORTH ELEVATION

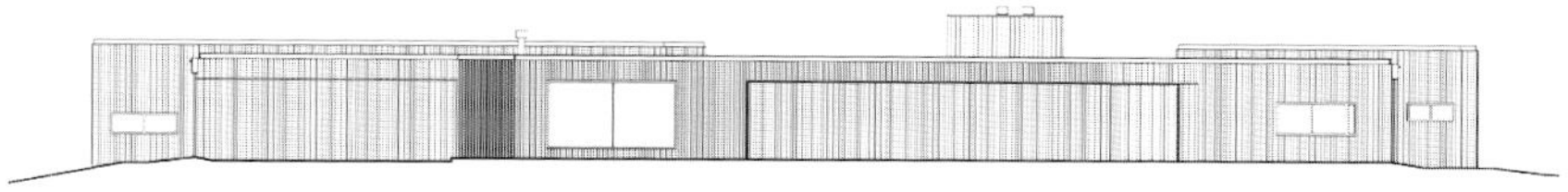

EAST ELEVATION

OPPOSITE The home's plan is laid out in wings around a sheltered courtyard containing a pool. Each wing offsets slightly to face a different aspect of the views. This makes each section feel separate from the other. The home is filled with secret doors opening both internally and externally.

The view can be enjoyed from the central pool
even in powerful on-shore winds.

PREVIOUS SPREAD, ABOVE AND OPPOSITE A wedge-shaped circulation with secret doors is created between different out-of-alignment wings. Horse riders from the local hunt often enjoy a refreshment in the motor court without dismounting. **PAGES 230-32** The house is in dialogue with the earth rampart archaeology of an ancient Māori *pā*, or fortified village, just discernible on the coastal razorback ridge in front.

HE TANGATA – IT IS PEOPLE

Once more:

What is the most important thing in the world?

He tangata, he tangata, he tangata.

It is people, it is people, it is people.

We are evolved beings. The planet has shaped who we are, but increasingly in the twenty-first century we are reshaping the planet; and in doing so we are reshaping ourselves and our descendants. This is more and more the imperative of the time we live in.

Initially, we felt it was enough to try to create good buildings, one at a time. Increasingly we have concluded that it is not that simple. There are bigger question to answer. What makes an environment a beautiful place? Why does that environment give us a sense of belonging? How does it make us happy? What is the influence it has on us?

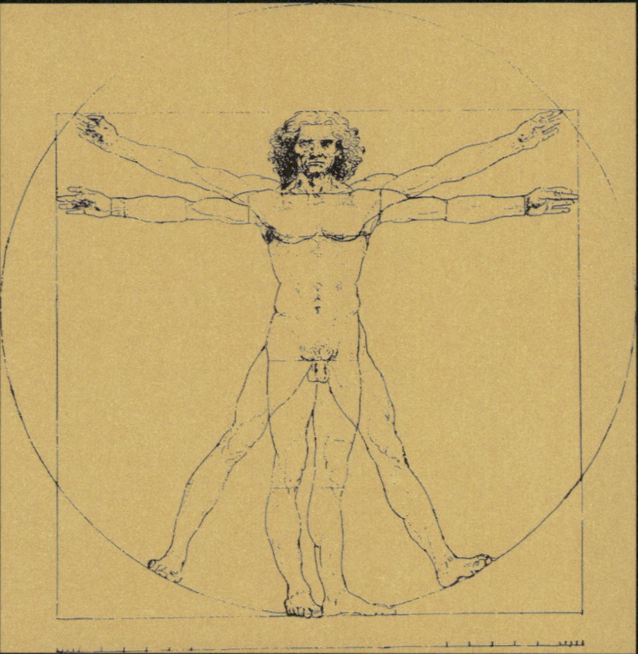

Such questions have long been the preoccupation of architecture, and th century we have been providing many answers. Urban design theory suggests that attraction is in a building's relationship with its urban environme the space around the building rather than the building itself making for successful design. Modern town planni deems an environment to be attractive when it is conforming to a certain bulk and use. Of course, style is the defining characteristic for others. Depending on preconceived taste, an individual predisposition towards brutalism, classicism or post-modernism informs our preferences. Beauty is in the eye of the beholder.

We are learning that the beauty of belonging and connection is ultimately about people and their environment. Architects in every culture have known this for centuries; classicists know that if you create a building in the proportion of the human body people will consider it beautiful. But people also admire other human attributes as well, for example the honesty of brutalism, the clarity of modernism, the familiarity of tradition.

As humans we are hard-wired to recognize and appreciate the human. It is often the clarity of the architect's consciousness seen in a finished work that gives us pleasure. That is why design by committee rarely produces beautiful architecture. Clear authorship is a key ingredient in beauty.

Leonardo da Vinci, *Vitruvian Man*, c.1490

HOW WE WORK

We are often asked why our houses all look so different when so many architects apply a similar design style to multiple clients and locations. It is because we approach our work as a unique collaboration between the clients, the site and ourselves.

To illustrate this, here are two examples from our current projects as we go to press: Glasshouse Rocks Pavilion is an aluminium and bronze beach pavilion, yet to be built, on Australia's New South Wales coast, and Wanaka House is under construction in Wanaka, New Zealand.

We start a project with a visit to the site with our clients. We know they have likely got to know the site well and have been thinking about the project for a long time, so we want to catch up.

Glasshouse Rocks Pavilion began with a site visit by float plane, landing at an isolated coastal farm, which is centred around the geologically significant Glasshouse Rocks - a local feature affectionally known as the shark and adze. It's here that the geology of New South Wales separates into black granite cliffs to the north and starkly contrasting soft white rock to the south. All of this set within a series of beautiful white-sand coves and crystal-clear lagoons. The clients, Justin and Kate, accommodated us in an old cottage and we swam, wandered and talked for 24 hours.

Before drawing anything, we always spend a lot of time talking with our clients about aspirations, favourite views, spatial relationships and area requirements, materials and durability, budgeting and energy efficiency. We ask them for some special words that sum up the home's feel. It's this process of meeting that is most helpful to us when designing a house. It can feel a little like being a hairdresser - we want their home to make our clients look and feel good.

This first step culminates in us (or our clients) writing up a detailed brief for the other to approve. In the case of Glasshouse Rocks Pavilion, a strong influence for Justin and Kate was the desire to regenerate the native forest that covered the land before its conversion to pasture in the eighteenth century. They saw their role as custodians rather than owners. The farm already contained several old cottages, but what was needed was a pavilion where people could meet, dine and watch a movie.

The aim of the brief is to define measurable tests for the success of the project, usually in three categories: aspirational, practical and human. These aims enable us and our clients to make design decisions that achieve the project's aims quickly and easily. For Glasshouse Rocks Pavilion these were -

1. to be the best place on the coast to watch a movie;
2. to leave the environment unchanged; and
3. to create a meeting point where everyone comes together naturally.

Glasshouse Rocks Pavilion is located on Australia's New South Wales coast. There is a cinema deep in the structure's shell and a large kitchen where people can gather. It has its own water reservoir and opens to a freshwater pool and a large lawn for children to play on. Just as a seashell amplifies the sound of the waves, the pavilion amplifies the experience of being on the beach. It is inspired by the experience of being in this place, and while it reflects its surroundings, it does so without trying to become part of the landscape.

obtuse
Acute
Basic shape of
fin

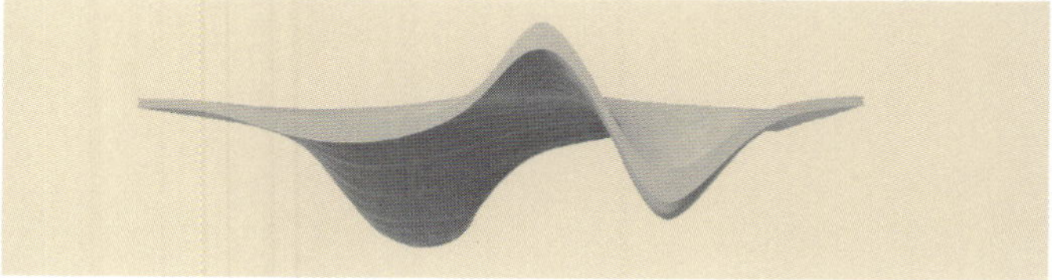

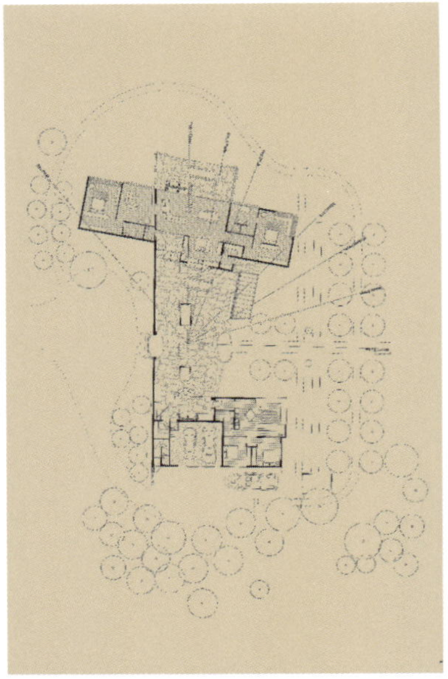

We start the drawing phase by producing 'bulk and location' diagrams that show the legislative requirements of the site, including density and height and yard limits. We also identify trees, possible views, positions of the sun, the effect of neighbours and future development plans.

Next we work on the preliminary design concept. This starts with a series of doodle-like drawings in the architect's sketchbook, which gradually develop into lifelike 3D renders.

For this project, we were captivated by the shark and adze and our first design used the geometry of the rocks to create a pavilion that matched. We raced back to Sydney to present our concept.

Justin and Kate hated it but they couldn't explain why. They were right. Our man-made rock would have ended up detracting from the beauty of nature's composition, which was already perfect.

We went back to the drawing board and this time were inspired by human experiences rather than the landscape: being on a beach, playing in the surf, collecting seashells, gathering round a fire with good food and the sound of the waves. What was needed was a home that had washed up here like a seashell and that didn't permanently alter the land. This time, Justin and Kate loved it.

Once the basic concept has been agreed, we develop the design into a CAD virtual model to estimate the construction cost. It's like looking through a lens - you see the bigger picture and then get more detailed with every set of drawings. The aim is to specify as much as possible about the building, so we can be accurate about its cost and it can be constructed in a streamlined process.

To address the challenge of the isolated location, we devised a way of prefabricating the pavilion as a single-piece welded-aluminium shell, in which most of the important sub-trades, including plumbing and electrics, can be factory-fitted and then shipped to the remote site.

Wanaka House is for a family who have spent many summers camping on this site. We got the concept design right the first time. At first glance, it's quite a conventional plan for a house and guest cottage, but the design has actually been subtly twisted to align the house to its mountaintop views. The mountains form a sequence of backdrops for everyday life in the house.

Once a preferred contractor is selected, we work as a team with the builder and draw up a construction contract between builder and client. We make regular site viists, check that quality is achieved and respond to queries. For example, the process of creating the charred, blackened-larch cladding for Wanaka House requires careful oversight. This oversight follows right through to the bottle of champagne and flowers on move-in day.

Wanaka House is located on the shore of Lake Wanaka on New Zealand's South Island. Its conventional plan - a home linked to a flat by a walkway - has been subtly twisted to align the house with the views of the surrounding mountaintops. This brings the experience of the environment into everyday life and provides a sense of belonging to the home's occupants.

BIOGRAPHIES

ANDREW PATTERSON, ARCHITECT

NZIA Gold Medal citation

Over the course of three decades Andrew Patterson has forged a reputation as a confident designer of striking buildings with great presence. His practice's portfolio is replete with distinctive projects. Patterson buildings do not just assert their difference against the designs of the architect's peers; they are also highly differentiated from each other. Consequently, Andrew's work epitomizes bespoke architecture and expresses the paradox of such particularity: he has generated a lineage uncharacterized by familial resemblance. He seems determined not to repeat himself.

That is not to say that Andrew's work is without defining traits or a common spirit. His architecture is as adventurous as he is aesthetically dexterous. He could surely turn his hand to any style, and like a high-art novelist dipping pseudonymously into genre writing, he has designed lesser-known works in a variety of idioms. But bold form-making is at the heart of Andrew's practice, along with an appreciation for and masterly deployment of materials. He likes the tough and solid stuff, especially concrete and steel.

This predilection is highly compatible with his declarative impulse. There is nothing tentative about Andrew's architecture. His is not a tread-lightly approach. Andrew's architecture is an architecture of occupation; buildings such as Site 3 (2001), Geyser (2012) and the Lodge at Kinloch Club (2016) take possession of their sites. Often, the buildings burrow in, as is the case with two Queenstown projects, AJ Hackett Bungy (2002) and the Michael Hill Golf Clubhouse (2008). Digging in, as Andrew points out, is not a foreign concept in this country; Māori were sculpting the earth in Aotearoa for centuries before the Europeans turned up.

Andrew is at least as comfortable talking about myths as about modernism. His attraction to mythologies, and the earth-moving and monument-making civilizations that have produced them, is expressed in strong formal statements such as Anvil and Local Rock House (both 2010) and the Len Lye Centre (2015). It also seems to feed his appetite for pattern-making, a hallmark of his architecture that is there for all to see on buildings as disparate as Cumulus (2003), Stratis (2005) and the Mai Mai house (2007). Pattern is not lightly applied to the façades of these buildings, but seemingly carved out of them. In Andrew's architecture clarity of concept is never betrayed by timidity of execution.

Unusually for a New Zealand architect, Andrew is not reticent about proclaiming his ambition and ability, or sharing his metaphorical excursions. The evocative nomenclature applied to many of his buildings – an amalgam of Platonic essentialism and capitalist branding – is a promise of excitement. As the late David Mitchell put it: 'Only an architect as courageous and skilled as Andrew can get away with fanning our expectations so flagrantly.' He gets away with it because his buildings consistently deliver on the promise of his concepts.

Andrew's potential was evident as a student – before he graduated he received the commission for his first house (at Karekare, completed in 1986) – and has been realized in a generation's worth of assured and often provocative buildings. The Summer Street House (1993), a Ponsonby 'urban bach' that substitutes steel wall for picket fence, was an early, and in this case literal, manifestation of his willingness to push the boundaries. Andrew's professional progress has been paved with architecture awards. All along, he has demonstrated an enviable facility for making the most of a project's design possibilities, and has long demonstrated a capacity to take a client along with him on an intrepid journey. He has a keen eye for talent; several of his senior staff have become significant practitioners in their own right. He has also gone where few New Zealand architects venture, into the big, wide world, designing, for example, the New Zealand Pavilion at the 2012 Frankfurt Book Fair and the New Zealand China Concept Store in Shanghai (2014).

Well into the middle part of his career, Andrew keeps growing, and his buildings keep surprising. Latterly, and significantly in post-earthquake Canterbury, his practice has applied a sensitive touch to the Christchurch Botanic Gardens Visitor Centre (2013) and dwellings (2013-2016) at Annandale on Banks Peninsula. Andrew is a singular figure in this country's architecture, a star following his own orbit. He is a most worthy winner of the New Zealand Institute of Architects Gold Medal.

The New Zealand Institute of Architects

PATTERSON ASSOCIATES

Andrew Patterson founded his eponymous architecture practice in 1986 and now leads it with his fellow directors Andrew Mitchell and Davor Popadich. Patterson designs for clients and sites globally but continues to be based in its studio, Luminous, in the heart of New Zealand's architecture district in Parnell, Auckland. Its work spans civic, commercial, exhibition and urban design, and of course residential.

Pattersons.com

SIMON DEVITT
(Photography, unless otherwise stated)

Simon Devitt is an Auckland-based photographer with a practice focus on architecture. His work is published in numerous national and international magazines, including *Elle Decor Italia*, *Architectural Digest* (Germany), *Dwell* (USA), *Habitus*, *InDesign* (Australia), *Architecture NZ*, *Urbis*, *Interior* (NZ).

Simon's images also feature in many books, including Julia Gatley's Auckland University Press-published *Long Live the Modern* (2009), *Group Architects: Towards a New Zealand Architecture* (2010) and *Athfield Architects* (2012). In 2013 Devitt launched his first self-published photo-book, *Portrait of a House*, on the Athfield residence in Wellington. He followed this in 2016 with *Rannoch*, about the life and home of New Zealand arts patron Sir James Wallace. *Rannoch* has gone on to win New Zealand photo-book of the year and won at the German Design Council Awards in 2018. Simon lectures in Photography of Architecture at the University of Auckland.

DAVOR POPADICH
(Photography: Northland Farmhouse and Millbrook)

Ranging across the disciplines of architecture, photography, and digital film and image, Davor Popadich's work engages with perceptions of space, nature, terrain and locality. Davor holds a Bachelor of Architecture degree with 1st class honours from the University of Auckland School of Architecture, and in 2013 he was admitted as a Fellow of the New Zealand Institute of Architects. Davor is a director at Patterson Associates and an inaugural member of the Board of Studies at the University of Auckland, School of Architecture. He lives and works in Auckland.

JENNY MARSHALL
(Interior Design: Seascape, Local Rock House, Millbrook and Waiheke)

Jenny Marshall trained and practised in interior design initially in London before returning to New Zealand in the late 1980s. Her passion is for texture and colour. Jenny's refined sense of luxury results in the creation of beautiful bespoke spaces that are tailored to each client. Jenny has collaborated with Patterson Associates on many projects, including Seascape, Local Rock House, Waiheke and Millbrook houses.

GLOSSARY OF MĀORI TERMS

Aotearoa
The Māori name for New Zealand. It is loosely translated as 'the land of the long white cloud'.

kaitiakitanga
Guardianship. Traditionally, Māori believe there is a deep kinship between humans and the natural world. This connection is expressed through *kaitiakitanga*.

marae
Courtyard of the tribal meeting house.

Ranginui and Papatūānuku
The Sky Father and the Earth Mother.

Te Ika-a-Māui
New Zealand's North Island.

Te Waipounamu
New Zealand's South Island.

whakapapa
Genealogy. *Whakapapa* links people to all other living things and to the earth and sky, and it traces the universe back to its origins.

wharenui
Meeting house, or main building of the *marae* where guests are greeted and accommodated.

ACKNOWLEDGMENTS

My sincere thanks to our clients, and particularly those who have generously allowed us to include their homes in this book.

Thank you to the consultants and contractors who we are lucky enough to work with to bring these projects to life.

Thank you to Tere Insley for reviewing the Māori content.

And a special thank you to my team at Patterson Associates. Thanks to my directors and associates Andrew Mitchell, Davor Popadich, Surya Fullerton, Shane Taylor and Luke Douglas, as well as to the team that worked on this book: Sajeev Ruthramoorthy, Emma Haughton, Kerry Marshall, Nicole Allan, George Grieve, David Moore, Patrick Sherwood and Michaella Franklin.

PICTURE CREDITS

All images are by Patterson Associates, unless otherwise noted below.

123RF Stock Photo: 234
Alexander Turnbull Library, Wellington, New Zealand: 20 (Ref: 1/1-003294-G), 21 (Ref: 1/2-116897-F), 72 (Ref: PUBL-0179-15), 124 (Ref: PA1-q-634-45-1), 125 (Ref: 1/2-051480-G)
Ed Cruikshank: 162
Danilo David: 240
Simon Devitt: 8-9, 13, 15, 18, 23-26, 32-38, 43, 46-53, 56-70, 75-78, 82-97, 100-112, 114, 116-22, 127, 142-45, 148-57, 158-59, 161, 164-74, 179-91, 204-05, 207-08, 210-17, 243, 248-49
Stephen Goodenough: 4-5, 54-55
Tim Gruchy: 232
Greg McKenzie: 30-31, 40-41
Jean-Luc Laloux: 218-22, 224-31
Davor Popadich: 128-30, 134-41, 192-203, 224L, 250-51
Patrick Reynolds: 16
David St. George: 242
David Straight: 115
Roberta Thornley: 243

On the front cover: Seascape Retreat (see page 26); on the back cover: Parihoa (see page 218)
Page 1: Andrew Patterson's first conceptual sketch for Mai Mai, 2006; Pages 4-5: Seascape Retreat; Pages 6-7: Wanaka House (under construction), render; Pages 8-9: Bethells Beach, view from the house; Pages 248-49: Bethells Beach; Pages 250-51: Dancers outside Len Lye Centre, New Plymouth

Designed by Steve Russell / aka-designaholic.com

First published in 2019 in the United States of America by Thames & Hudson Inc., 500 Fifth Avenue, New York, New York 10110

www.thamesandhudsonusa.com

Library of Congress Control Number 2018945300

ISBN 978-0-500-022191

Printed in China by Shanghai Offset Printing Products Limited